25·12·1991.

Happy Christmas Mum,
             lots of lov

xxx Simon xx

BELOVED QUIXOTE

BELOVED QUIXOTE

The Unknown Life
of John Middleton Murry

by

KATHERINE MIDDLETON MURRY

But pray sir, what is it you mean to do in this
fag-end of the world?
Sancho Panza to Don Quixote

A CONDOR BOOK
SOUVENIR PRESS (E & A) LTD

To Johnnie and Marie

First published 1986 by Souvenir Press (Educational and Academic) Ltd, 43 Great Russell Street, London WC1B 3PA and simultaneously in Canada

ISBN 0 285 65027 0

Photoset in Great Britain by
Rowland Phototypesetting Ltd,
Bury St Edmunds, Suffolk
Printed in Great Britain by
Billing & Sons Ltd, Worcester

Acknowledgements

The events described in Part I of this book are taken largely from my father's own writings, both published and unpublished, and to a lesser extent from his conversations with me in later years. For Part II I have drawn freely on my own childhood memories, and on my father's unpublished Journals which he wrote continuously throughout that time.

Quotations from my father's writings and those of other authors, and references to specific events, are acknowledged in the footnotes. Unless otherwise stated, published works cited are by John Middleton Murry.

I should like to convey my sincere thanks to The Authors Society as the literary representative of the Estate of John Middleton Murry and to my brother, J. C. Middleton Murry, as Literary Executor, for permission to publish extracts from my father's Journals and to quote from his published books. The letter from Katherine Mansfield to Princess Elizabeth Bibesco (p. 40) is also reprinted by permission of The Authors Society © the Estate of John Middleton Murry and was previously published by Antony Alpers in *The Life of Katherine Mansfield* (1980, Viking Press). I am grateful to Laurence Pollinger Ltd and the Estate of Mrs Frieda Lawrence Ravagli for allowing me to quote from D. H. Lawrence's *Fantasia of the Unconscious*.

Lastly, my deep gratitude to my editor, Tessa Harrow, for all her valuable advice and patient encouragement.

KMM

Contents

List of Illustrations

Prologue

The tragic events which I relate in this book had many of their roots in D. H. Lawrence's unrequited passion for my father, John Middleton Murry, and in my father's idealisation of his first wife, Katherine Mansfield. Long after his death in 1930 Lawrence's influence upon 'the raven', as he called my father, continued to colour my childhood and adult years, as did my father's own intense love for Katherine Mansfield who died in 1923, two years before I was born.

These two dead writers of great talent continued to run like mysterious rivers through my father's soul. I saw how absolutely and heroically he kept faith with them as he perfected and embellished into an ideal woman Katherine Mansfield's own projection of herself, and extended Lawrence's demand for 'blood brotherhood' with him into many a personal effort to achieve the brotherhood of Man.

Children, monies, health and reputation were sacrificed before my eyes in his perpetual quest for what was true for himself, and therefore (he reasoned) for Mankind.

As a child I had a book bound in crimson with gold letters, *The Story of Don Quixote.* Inside was a picture of the knight charging at a row of windmills that receded into the distance. I liked him and liked his old horse Rosinante, and Sancho Panza following behind. There was something comfortingly familiar about him, funny and sad and lone, more real than any of the other fairytale Knights of the Round Table.

And like Quixote, my father always seemed to be one against the many. During raging domestic storms I would look on in mute and passionate support for this embattled knight of mine. With smouldering indignation I watched his contemporaries retire in safety to the sidelines. My haughty disdain for them I kept to myself. When it came to *real* sacrifices, what did they know, I thought? Were they not all, yes all, the lesser men?

These things I knew in my heart as a child and watched with tears during my youth. In adult years I tried to forget—for such was the pain—until I could carry on no more with this pit of darkness in my soul. So I attempted to discover the reasons for the tragedy from which my father, to the despair of his brother and friends, could not be deflected. I began by searching his early years, seeking in them the seeds of the later disaster in which I, throughout my childhood, was to be a helpless, fearful participant.

PART I

PRELUDE

1

Lawrence

As a young man my father won a scholarship in Classics to Oxford, but abandoned what had promised to be a brilliant academic career in order to live in London with Katherine Mansfield and support himself as a journalist. It was one year after this, in 1913, that he and D. H. Lawrence first met.

Lawrence had been asked to contribute to *The Blue Review*, a literary magazine my father and Katherine were editing, and had called in at the office in London. Their contact was, as my father later told me, 'immediate and overwhelming'.

At that time the two men were both living with married women, which in those days was socially unacceptable. Lawrence had eloped with Frieda, the wife of his Professor of French at Nottingham University, while Katherine had left her husband, a teacher of Divinity in London.

So Katherine and Frieda, Lawrence and Murry found they had more in common than literature alone. Moreover the women were both 'foreigners'. Frieda was the daughter of a wealthy German aristocrat and Katherine came from a prosperous New Zealand family. As for Lawrence and Murry, both as English as the English soil itself, they were *déracinés*. Lawrence was the son of a miner and Murry of a clerk in the lower ranks of the Civil Service. The one had thrown up his teaching post, the other his university.

The sight of them together must have been arresting: Katherine dark and petite and Murry with his classically handsome features; easy-going, golden-haired Frieda and the gawky, fiery Lawrence.

We have glimpses of them in those carefree days before the First World War as they rode together in a London bus, to lunch in Soho or to a party at H. G. Wells', with Lawrence excessively proud of his first dress suit and Murry wearing cuff-links they had made from buttons and beer-bottle wire.*

But their whereabouts are less easy to follow. The Murrys flitted from England to France, the Lawrences from Germany to Italy. They stayed in modest rooms, cheap hotels and damp country cottages. Lawrence could write his novels anywhere, as could Katherine, with the freedom her allowance gave her, while Frieda did not mind where she was. For Murry, however, despite his inclination, comparative stability was something of a necessity, since he was obliged to earn his living on the London newspapers.

In 1914 Lawrence and Frieda were married, with Murry a witness at the registry office. It was to be another four years before Katherine would obtain her divorce.

However, between Frieda and Lawrence, as with Katherine and Murry, life was by no means unmitigated dove-cooing. Katherine was often discontented and restless and Frieda angered Lawrence when she grieved for the children she had abandoned.

'Perhaps you will come into possession of your own soul,' Lawrence had written to Murry from Italy, 'when this affair of you and Katherine has gone crash.'† Murry felt he could have said the same about Lawrence, who was already rather too inclined to take charge of him . . .

In August 1914, a month after the Lawrences' marriage, war broke out between England and Germany.

Murry enlisted in the territorials but was rejected on medical grounds. Frieda found herself an enemy alien in England, and Katherine's only and much loved brother joined up (only to be killed eight months later). Lawrence vehemently abhorred the whole political and military scene.

Unlike their contemporaries of the Bloomsbury Group who, they felt, went on with their sheltered lives as if the War were simply not happening, they were profoundly affected; nothing for them could ever have the old insouciance again.

In imagination, but in imagination only, they would all escape from the War to an island they called *Rananim*. Lawrence expounded on the new spirit of life they would live there, Murry

---

* In those days beer bottles were hand corked and the corks held fast with wire, like champagne corks.

† Mentioned in *Between Two Worlds*, 1935 (Cape), p. 280.

D. H. Lawrence's phoenix symbol.

invented the ship with Lawrence's phoenix as her sail and Katherine dreamed of the brightly coloured bundles they would each carry. A beautiful day-dream.*

After Christmas Katherine, who had been encouraging love-letters from Francis Carco, one of Murry's French writer friends, went off and joined him behind the Front in France. Much to Lawrence's indignation Murry made no attempt to prevent her. During her absence the Lawrences asked him over to Sussex where they were staying.

He arrived ill with influenza. It was Lawrence, not Frieda, who put him to bed and nursed him like a child; his tenderness seemed to have no limits. But on the third day, Murry recalled,† Lawrence 'opened fire'. He railed at Murry for his association with one of his working colleagues, then accused him of being responsible for Katherine's departure: he was too weak with her and, besides, she felt excluded from his intellectual discussions with his men friends. But Murry, lonely as he was without her, nevertheless maintained that she should be free, since freedom was the essence of love.

* Described by Frieda Lawrence in *Not I but the Wind*, 1935 (Heinemann), p. 79.

† Recorded in *Between Two Worlds*, Chap. 23. The colleague referred to by Lawrence was Gordon Campbell, with whom my father would hold long philosophical discussions.

There followed some confused talk. Together they would start the Revolution and lay the foundations of their new society; the present one was corrupt and had led to the War. That much they agreed upon.

But when Lawrence declared that he wanted to kill one million, two million Germans in revenge for the war-machine they had unleashed, Murry was shocked. This was a far cry from the *Rananim* he had imagined.

His shock became mystification when Lawrence insisted that Murry's 'effort was purer' than his own, and then distinct unease when his friend stated that the 'angel of himself' would rise out of the 'animal in himself'.*

That Murry cherished Lawrence's friendship is beyond doubt, but when he sensed that Lawrence required more of him, he recoiled.

He was twenty-four at the time and Lawrence twenty-eight.

Katherine returned from France, disillusioned with Carco. Not that she wanted to come back to Murry, she said, he need not think that, it was just that she had nowhere else to go (Ida Baker, her college friend—LM† as she called her—was away in Rhodesia). Typically Murry, instead of congratulating himself on the demise of his rival, comforted Katherine in her disappointment.

Now reconciled, the Murrys left their uncomfortable country cottage for Hampstead to run a new paper, *The Signature*, with Lawrence. Its lifespan was brief. Then Murry was given a permanent post as reviewer on *The Times Literary Supplement*, which at last gave him a measure of freedom. A few months later he and Katherine left England for the South of France.

They went to Marseilles and from there explored the coast and eventually settled in Bandol. There, blissfully happy at the Villa Pauline, they worked at the same table. Katherine wrote *Prelude* and Murry a study of Dostoevsky.‡ They lived frugally, the only luxuries they could afford being dates and honey.

The Lawrences, meanwhile, had gone down to Cornwall where, only a stone's throw from their rented cottage, they saw the *very place* for the Murrys, with a kind of tower room for Katherine to

* *Between Two Worlds*, pp. 333–6.
† Leslie Moore, Ida Baker's pseudonym.
‡ *Dostoevsky: A Critical Study*, 1916 (Martin Secker).

write in. Letters were despatched forthwith to Bandol entreating their friends to join them in starting a community at Higher Tregerthen which was 'like a little monastery'.* Murry warmed to the idea although he hesitated when he saw Katherine so aghast. But when Lawrence went on to cry, 'Out of the disciples there was one Judas!',† Murry was unable to hold out.

At the beginning of April 1916 the Murrys left the Villa Pauline. As they closed the gate behind them Katherine was in tears.

*   *   *

Even in the spring Katherine disliked Cornwall. It seemed to her all boulders. As for the hamlet near Zennor that the Lawrences had chosen, she hated it on sight. The wind blew and she stamped her foot in exasperation. Auspices, or 'aspegs' as she called them, were not good.

For his own part Murry would have been happy enough. He relished his walks with Lawrence as the two men, shouldering rucksacks, set off together to St Ives where they bought cheap furniture at the fishermen's sales.

Together as they scrubbed and painted they planned their new society, this brotherhood in which the men in their 'male purpose' would be followed by their women.

Katherine, who did not want to follow anybody, felt left out. She sulked and smoked endless cigarettes up in her room, meditating cynical stories.

Frieda, as she cooked and polished and arranged vases of fox-gloves, was not to be put down either; she went so far as to contradict Lawrence when he began denouncing Shelley. Lawrence, who hated intellectual women, exploded.

The Revolution, he had insisted, should include a new sexual awareness between man and woman. But when the Murrys, with mounting embarrassment, witnessed the Lawrences' violent quarrels, fresh from their own idyllic happiness at the Villa Pauline, they felt that Lawrence had not much to teach them in these matters. Katherine privately called Lawrence's house 'The Phallus'.

Jealous of Katherine, Lawrence pressed Murry for a more inti-

* D. H. Lawrence to John Middleton Murry, February 1916.
† D.H.L. to J.M.M., 18th March, 1916.

mate relationship. The more Murry timidly but unequivocally withdrew, the more Lawrence sought to bind him to him in 'blood brotherhood', which was to be an 'inviolable sacrament'.

The younger man took this to be a sort of ceremony in black magic to be performed on the eerie Cornish moors. He enquired naïvely:

'If I love you and you know I love you, isn't that enough?'

Evidently it was not: there had to be blood-mingling.

'I hate your love, I *hate* it!' was Lawrence's tortured response.

And so Murry took refuge in his propensity for long intellectual discussions which Lawrence countered by retreating into a mindless world of his own.*

It is small wonder that after two months Katherine was even less enthusiastic for Cornwall and communal life than before. She and Murry decided to part company with the Lawrences. Murry took his bicycle and went off in search of another place for them both and found a cottage on the warmer southern coast at Mylor.

When they broke their news Lawrence pretended indifference. But they were not deceived. 'They should have a soft valley,' he wrote bitterly to Lady Ottoline Morrell, 'with leaves and the ring-dove cooing.'†

He was then seized with bouts of delirium, rocking and moaning at nights, calling Murry an 'obscene bug' that was 'sucking his life away'.‡

On the Murrys' last day at Higher Tregerthen, Katherine left by train and Murry hired a driver with a horse and cart for their belongings. Lawrence helped load the furniture and tie it down. When Murry said his final farewell Frieda was cheerful and sure they would all meet again soon. But Lawrence stood back, silent. The men's hearts were sore. Murry was only too aware of the depth of their rift as he wheeled his bicycle along the track and rode away, following the horse and cart, to Katherine at Mylor.

*   *   *

Murry had rejected Lawrence for Katherine. But the break between the two men was far from final; they needed one another too much.

*   *Reminiscences of D. H. Lawrence*, 1933 (Cape), p. 79.
†   D. H. Lawrence to Lady Ottoline Morrell, 24th May, 1916.
‡   *Between Two Worlds*, p. 416.

From Mylor Murry took up a London post in the Intelligence Department of the War Office. It was in December of the following year that Katherine's tuberculosis was first diagnosed and she was advised to go to the South of France.

The Lawrences, suspected of signalling from their cottage to German submarines, were expelled from Cornwall as spies. Confined to England, with the suppression of his novel *The Rainbow* three years earlier still rankling, Lawrence could not get published and felt cold-shouldered by the literary establishment. The failure of his relationship with Murry compounded his bitterness; he could not wait to shake the dust of England off his feet. He was engaged in writing *Women in Love* at the time, which he had begun when the Murrys were in Cornwall although he had kept quiet about it to them. Murry was not to know of its existence until it was published in 1921, and even then he did not realise when and in what circumstances it had been written. (Furthermore, the suppressed Prologue where Lawrence, through his characters, made his attraction for his 'dark-haired' male friends perfectly plain, was suppressed until 1968, more than ten years after Murry's death.)*

In 1919 the Lawrences were finally able to leave England and Katherine was never to see them again. They went to Italy and then to America via Australia and New Zealand. But they did not lose touch. When Katherine was at Fontainebleau seeking a cure for her tuberculosis, Murry wrote to Lawrence 'suggesting, I suppose, that our relationship should be renewed'. By the time Lawrence's reply came from America ('Heaven knows what we all are, and how we should feel if we met now that we are all changed: we'll have to meet and see'), Katherine had died. When he heard the news, deeply affected, Lawrence wrote to Murry that they 'would unite up again' when he came to England.†

Meanwhile, in 1923, Lawrence sent him his book *Fantasia of the Unconscious* which was to influence him so profoundly and wherein Lawrence asked some man to join him in creating a new world. Murry decided forthwith to start a new magazine which would lay the foundations of this new world and be a mouthpiece for himself and Lawrence when he came back. He cabled to Lawrence in New

* See Antony Alpers, *The Life of Katherine Mansfield*, 1980 (Viking Press).
† *Reminiscences of D. H. Lawrence*, pp. 104–5.

Mexico for permission to publish *Fantasia*. Lawrence agreed and *The Adelphi** began its life with the essential chapters of *Fantasia* published in England for the first time.

But Lawrence vacillated over his return. He went to buy a ticket to England, then did not. Murry was nonplussed. Once again, as with *Women in Love*, he did not know that *Fantasia* had been written three years previously and that Lawrence had now changed.

In the autumn of that same year Frieda, disenchanted with Lawrence and his Mexican moods, left him to visit Europe. On his way to Freiburg to consult a doctor on behalf of T. S. Eliot's wife, Vivien, Murry travelled with her.

Then Lawrence finally did come to England. When Murry met him at the station he looked very ill and almost the first enigmatic words he uttered were: 'I can't bear it.'† He said that *The Adelphi* should attack everything and explode in one blaze of denunciation and insisted that Murry return with him to New Mexico because he needed him badly. They would create their nucleus of the new society over there.

At first Murry agreed, but then he changed his mind. His reasons were several: he felt strongly that their new society should be in England that had suffered the War and not Mexico which would just be an escape for moneyed people. He had other private reasons, too: Dorothy Brett was to join them in Mexico, which would be an embarrassment for, after Katherine's death, she had been certain of marrying Murry, who was not in love with her. On the other hand, he and Frieda had fallen for each other, but he had discouraged Frieda's advances when they had travelled together, out of loyalty to Lawrence who was ill and dependent on his wife.

So Lawrence and Frieda returned together to New Mexico with Dorothy Brett but without Murry, and each man felt he had been let down by the other.

However, shortly before this departure a crucial event had taken place. It was during a supper at the Café Royal. Gathered round the table with other friends, Murry, for the first and last time, leaned

---

*   *The Adelphi*, whose title means 'the brotherhood', ran from 1923 to 1948. D. H. Lawrence's *Fantasia of the Unconscious* was subsequently published by Martin Secker in 1930 in the New Adelphi Library.

†   *Son of Woman*, 1931 (Cape), p. 331.

over to Lawrence and kissed him and said: 'I love you, Lorenzo, but I cannot promise never to betray you!'*

Other people there have given their versions of this strange scene, but in fact there were only two people who knew the meaning of those words: Murry and Lawrence. The former was to explain that moment only after Lawrence's death. He said that he had had a sudden praeternatural illumination and in a flash knew Lawrence's secret. In an unpremeditated gesture of profound pity and love he had leaned over and kissed his friend, and at that moment knew beyond all doubt that Lawrence had understood him and knew that he knew.

The secret was, I am absolutely convinced, Lawrence's homosexuality. Taboo in those days, it was Lawrence's tragedy in which Murry was powerless to help. He could only look on while his beloved friend, capable of such depths of love beneath all the venom and hatred, was cut off in a no-man's-land, to live out an agony, lonely beyond all remedy.

Beyond veiled words, 'for those that have ears to hear',† Murry never betrayed Lawrence's secret.

They saw each other again when they both felt 'the pain of the old affection more deeply. But manifestly there was nothing to be done'. As ever, they disputed, quarrelled and became reconciled. Then, in May 1929, Murry learned that Lawrence was seriously ill, that it was only a matter of months. He 'felt a great longing to see him again before he died'‡ and proposed to go to Majorca where he then was. But Lawrence replied that 'it was no good' their meeting: 'Even when we are immortal spirits we shall dwell in different Hades.'§

*   *   *

'He'll build the temple if I carve out the way . . .' Lawrence had written to Lady Ottoline Morrell. 'Murry is one of the men of the future.'¶ He was only too correct. As a child I lived in one 'temple' after another. As one collapsed, my father, in his perpetual search for what was good for Mankind, bravely built up another. Thus

---

* *Reminiscences of D. H. Lawrence*, p. 175.
† *Idem*, p.24.
‡ *Idem*, pp. 119–123.
§ D. H. Lawrence to John Middleton Murry, 20th May, 1929.
¶ D. H. Lawrence to Lady Ottoline Morrell, February 1915.

Jack—

Will the bird perish,
Shall the bird rise.

To the old raven, in
the act of becoming a
young phœnix

D H L

*Enlarged impression of a seal given by D. H. Lawrence to John
Middleton Murry at Christmas, 1923, with Lawrence's accompanying
note.*

Lawrence's phoenix was always to rise from the ashes, but, alas, my experience was almost entirely of the ashes. The wings of fledglings are tender. So I grew up trying to protect my father from these disasters, these 'Rananims', these experiments in communal living, and from the effects of his third marriage with the 'earth-woman' (another untried ideal of Lawrence), the violent, raging Betty, who screamed out her obscenities for ten long years.

At the end, when he had ruined his health and shortened his life, he pronounced that Lawrence was nearly right. Never was a little word, so anodyne in itself, more loaded with tragedy than that 'nearly'.

2

Katherine

The other influence upon my father, that of Katherine Mansfield, was infinitely subtle and pervasive because it was the influence of a dead woman.

In my present solitude, I see how the myth and the mysterious presence of Katherine Mansfield, of my father's love for her and hers for him, determined the very landscape of the soul with which I was born.

Why it is now and only now that I can recognise these presences for what they are I do not know. Perhaps all things have their appointed time to be transformed from poor ghosts haunting us and full of pain into benign and resplendent realities. Perhaps it is better not to ask questions, simply to accept.

As I watch the morning mist roll away and build itself up again into huge cloud-mountains, they seem like the snows of the past, enveloping in a cacoon a young man and his wife, in Switzerland in the autumn of 1921.

At Montana-sur-Sierre, wrapped in quietness, hemmed in by pine trees weighted with snow, their Chalet des Sapins is slipping gently into late afternoon as the lengthening sunbeams lie low over its roof.

The young woman, Katherine Mansfield, is in her room upstairs, lying on her bed. Rather small and so thin that her wedding ring slides up and down her finger and her collar-bones protrude knife-like beneath her Jaeger woollen dress, her transparent, wax-like complexion, small pursed mouth which would need much to make it tremble, small, slightly retroussé nose, brown hair brushed straight and cut short with a fringe in the Chinese style, neat, carefully manicured hands curved inwards as if they were holding some fragile vase, all give her the faintly exotic air of an oriental doll. Her eyes seem to be ever darkening and dusted over with faint red gold as they measure up the world severely, judging, missing nothing; while, clinging to the very folds of the rug that covers her, is the dull sound of her cough. Beside her is her journal where she notes, 'The deep grudge LM has for me really is fascinating . . .'*

Down below in the porch, the young man, John Middleton Murry, careful not to disturb his invalid wife, cheerfully knocks the snow off his boots and comes indoors with a long, rolling gait. Strikingly handsome, ruddy and bronzed from the sun's strong rays, he deposits his skates with a kind of respect, peels off his jacket and gloves and rubs his swollen elbows under his sweater as he warms himself over the stove. Then he catches sight of a small parcel dangling on a black thread over his balcony. He smiles at this present from his 'Tig' in the room above to her 'Bogey' down below. It consists of one yellow envelope, one cigarette and one 1.20 centimes Swiss stamp. He sits down at his writing table, lights the cigarette and sticks the stamp, 'so that it shall not be desecrated by the post', into his large army notebook.†

With unusually beautiful eyes he seems to be looking always inwards. Ten months younger than his wife Katherine, he is barely thirty-one. Oblivious of his charm, unaffected by his looks, diffident and shy, he often describes himself as a 'queer fish'‡ or worse, a 'dead cabbage . . . something very tight and yellow with a faintly unpleasant smell'.§

His table is strewn with books and papers. A biography of Dostoevsky, Goethe's *Conversations with Eckermann* in the German text, *Stendhal et ses Commentateurs* in which he has underlined *l'action de créer exige de la force* and *le corps et la tête sont les valêts de l'âme.*

In view of his deprecatory remarks about himself, one would hardly believe that he is among the up-and-coming bright young men of the time. In fact he has won the OBE for his work as Chief Censor during the War; presented Proust and Gide to the English

* *The Journal of Katherine Mansfield: Definitive Edition, 1904–1922,* edited by John Middleton Murry, 1954 (Constable), October 1921.
† Undated entry in manuscript notebook.
‡ A self-deprecating description my father often applied to himself.
§ *The Things We Are,* 1922 (Constable), p. 154.

public; established his reputation as a literary critic; delivered a series of lectures on literary style at Oxford, and at last earned enough money to be able to spend a few months in Switzerland. So it is with a light heart yet with a typical wry, wondering, Chaplinesque ruefulness that he writes in his notebook:

> Why do I fall down more often and more heavily than anyone else skating on the lake? Today I bruised both elbows, both hips, my right knee and sprained my right ankle in trying to do an outside edge. I feel that I appear as 'a small figure gesticulating wildly on the sky-line'. I seem to hear the Swiss natives saying: '*Voyez cet homme qu'il est extra-ordinaire.*' '*C'est un anglais,*' says another, explaining everything. At that thought I get up from the ice and try to look as if I had been practising not an outside edge but how to fall . . .*

The sound of Tig's cough upstairs casts a gloom over his spirits. It is the 'snail under the leaf', as she would say. One of them. There is another: Ida Baker, the ungainly LM. Until recently she has been living at the chalet, ministering to Katherine's needs and looking after Wingley, their black and white cat. LM, this passionately devoted slave, Katherine calls 'my wife',† but then Katherine has also described herself as 'more than half a man'‡ and now she is an invalid, demanding, spoilt and often cruel. She rules as sick people and children sometimes do when they make others pay for their weakness, exacting as they do this a terrible toll.

LM, one of the few women not to throw herself about his neck, resents Katherine's young husband, this man about the house, to be fed and kept warm, this intruder coming for ever between Katherine and herself. And who can ever understand Katherine's needs as well as LM? But sadly for LM, it is she who is *de trop* and, with pain in her heart, she has left the chalet and rented a room in the village where she has found work at one of the clinics.

Today, as every day when she has finished, she comes to look after her Katherine, prepare her little dishes, wash and mend her clothes, sew buttons on Katherine's velvet jackets and ribbons on

---

* Undated entry in manuscript notebook.
† Katherine Mansfield to the Hon. Dorothy Brett, 1922. Quoted by Antony Alpers in *The Life of Katherine Mansfield,* 1980 (Viking Press).
‡ *The Journal of Katherine Mansfield,* 1st June, 1907.

her crêpe-de-chine underclothes. Ernestine, the Swiss maidservant, is too heavy-handed to do such things.

Murry and Katherine are talking and laughing together. Katherine has imagined that Wingley keeps a journal, too, in which he calls her 'Granma Jaeger', Murry 'Master and Man', Ernestine 'The Swede' and LM 'The Foster-Monger', but that he is very puzzled because he cannot understand why Foster-Monger has no *box* of her own . . .*

At evenfall Murry and Katherine go out for a short, slow walk, as far as Katherine can go. A house they pass by with its windows lit up is full of soldiers. One of them is playing an accordion—beautifully. Together they stand and listen until he stops. Could they have been so deeply affected by Beethoven? The simple, obvious dance music seems somehow to be life itself as though it were just caught up—naked, real, and for ever unalterable.

And then, long after the music has stopped and Katherine has retired to bed, Murry, reading *Julius Caesar*, comes to Brutus' farewell:

> For ever and for ever farewell, Cassius!
> If we do meet again, why we shall smile;
> If not, why then this parting was well made.

and it seems to him that it is the same as the music: not art, nearer to life than art can ever get. Sad and beautiful; but not intoxicating, no leading away from us giving a glimpse beyond; no reconciliation, no recollection even. But the very living life itself—passing and caught as it passes.

LM, who is filling hot water bottles for Katherine, slides them between the sheets. She has lately had a tempting offer of work at a mission hospital in India where she had lived as a child. The woman who asked her to become house-mother for the home out there could not understand why Ida should refuse in order to stay with Katherine. But then how was she to know of the emotional bond between the two women? Of Katherine's fierce possessiveness? And the pathetic, adoring LM, used and cast aside at Katherine's whim, tolerated at best by Murry, more often simply ignored or, worse, *not even seen* by him, has doubtless never heard of lesbianism.

* Undated entry in manuscript notebook.

Katherine and Murry are playing cribbage. They have been discussing a certain X who is having treatment in the nearby sanatorium and had visited them and praised a contemporary writer. Katherine had torn the author to shreds. The visitor, confused, had weakly agreed with her. When he has gone, Murry roundly concludes that such men like tripe and would eat it at the tripe shop if they dared. But, since they do not, the stuff has to be wrapped up in coloured tissue paper with a bow of ribbon . . . and how can such a man, one of the 10,000 intelligent men in England —understand Chekhov? What chance have they, Murry and Katherine, who are trying to go on from Chekhov? Moral: don't depend on writing for a living!*

Chekhov's art and his morality are to be their guide. A few weeks earlier, Katherine had finished *The Garden Party* and *The Doll's House*. Murry, discovering his strengths, is preparing another series of critical essays. He prophesies that the year's winner of the Hawthornden Prize for which Katherine's *Bliss* has been turned down, will be forgotten ten years hence and it is Katherine's *Prelude* that will be remembered . . .

LM, full of hurt at being excluded by these two lovers, indignantly maintains that Murry's ideas are really Katherine's anyway. But LM's moment here in Montana is still to come . . .

*   *   *

Clouds were beginning to gather. Katherine was growing restless again. It was the same old story: the chalet and its surroundings had started off brilliantly, then they began to pall. She could no longer bear the snow, or the Swiss, or the mountains.

She complained. Her health was not improving fast enough. She wrote to her Russian friend and admirer, Kot (Samuel Koteliansky), translator of Chekhov and other Russian authors—'Shmul', as Lawrence and the others often called him. From his rooms in London, he answered her with sympathy. Had she heard of a certain Dr Manoukhin, established in Paris, who used a new treatment with rays, especially beneficial for tuberculosis?†

Katherine mentioned this to Murry who could not conceal his

---

* Recorded in manuscript notebook.
† See Antony Alpers, *The Life of Katherine Mansfield.*

misgivings. Where bodily health was concerned, there was always to be in this romantic much common sense. He reminded her that life in the mountains, with its quiet and regular routine, was keeping the consumption at bay. She had been able to work, too. Besides, they were together . . .

Ill as she was, perhaps he sensed, too, that the Chalet des Sapins was to be the last place of real happiness and tranquillity they were to know together.

But Kot had sown the seed. Katherine continued to write to him. For the rest of his life Murry would curse Kot for being a 'blundering and interfering fool' and remember how a friend had said to him once: 'You call Kot a great rock. I call him a bloody mule.'*

When Kot died in 1955, Murry's description of him in his journal was full of sympathy and admiration: for his devotion to Katherine; for this 'sort of Moses' with his high and strict moral code and contempt for the money-grubber, the wide-boy, such people as Gertler's family; full of pity, too, for a Kot with his 'pathetically extravagant notions of the power and prestige of literature', who wanted to run a magazine† 'as big as a telephone book'. But that was later . . .

Now, by another stroke of misfortune, Orage, editor of *The New Age*, posted *Cosmic Anatomy* by a friend of his for Murry to review. Murry, sceptical as he was ever to be of theosophism and the occult, had little time for it. But Katherine devoured the book. Indeed, could this not be the very answer to her predicament? Could it not be her impure self that was holding her body back from recovery? Why, she wondered, was Murry so set against these doctrines?

In the face of Murry's misgivings, she secretly confided in LM and enlisted her help in a scheme she was hatching: the two women would both go to Paris where Katherine could consult Dr Manoukhin. LM, indulgent to the point of folly, convinced that Murry did not understand her Katherine's real needs, readily complied. Bags would be packed, train seats booked and 'Jack' could stay behind to get on with his 'selfish' pursuits.

Murry, with a trustfulness and blindness to plotting females which was to become legendary in our family, in all probability

* Journal, 1955.
† *The Adelphi*.

quite unaware of what was going on in Katherine's room upstairs or even how fatally Katherine was turning away from him, confided in his notebook on Christmas Day, 1921:

> What will the year bring forth? . . . I don't think my lack of success seriously perturbs me. James Joyce has liberated too much, opened too many horizons—so I feel now—for me to worry about such things. No, I ask for a share of cheap, ordinary, commonplace happiness; the most ordinary quality, 6¾d a yard. A child, for instance; a little house of my own, of *our* own; above all, the condition of all these things, that Tig should be no longer an absolute invalid. I cannot reconcile myself to this utterly frustrated life. I can bear it, I suppose; but I wake every morning to perpetual rebellion. Tig's cough in the morning pulls the shutters down on the day for me. It can never be real sunlight afterwards, for I know that I am only half-alive. Can I put faith in an omen? Today Tig had her long-awaited letter from Dr Manoukhin. Today! Well, I can't help thinking of what will be in my mind when I read this next Christmas. This would be the moment for prayer.

His Tig had barely a year to live.

*   *   *

LM and Katherine left for Paris as they had planned. Murry joined them when he had finished the work he was engaged upon. LM returned to the chalet to close it up and take Wingley back to England. In Paris, Murry and Katherine, now sought-after in literary circles, met the Russian colony there; also James Joyce, Paul Valéry and others. Paris was still Paris of the *guignols* and the café-concerts, the place, too, where Murry had met his first love, Madeleine, whom, characteristically, he was never to forget; the Paris of Carco whose later literary embroidery of his relationship with Katherine Murry found a shocking travesty of the facts.*

The sessions with Manoukhin were a disaster. He turned out to be the quack doctor Murry had suspected and Katherine, at sight of him, also began to doubt. Extremely weakened by the whole Paris venture, she returned to Switzerland with Murry, her mind more

* Journal, 1955.

and more set on a different cure. Murry could not believe that she
was taking the right course and could not bring himself to pretend
to believe in order to please her. Katherine sent for LM from
London and, with her usual devotion, LM arrived. Then, after two
months, all three of them travelled back to London where Katherine, a living skeleton but more than ever bent on her new psychic
cure, embraced Orage and Koteliansky and attended Ouspensky's
lectures. In a letter to Koteliansky she wrote that she was 'deeply
sorry for Murry', although she was 'determined to remain his friend
and to make him free of his own will. Special cases need special
methods . . .'* while Murry afterwards wrote: 'I could scarcely bear
to discuss the doctrines of Ouspensky with Katherine. The gulf
between us was painful to us both and living under the same roof
became a kind of torture . . .'†

So he went away to live in the country, at the house of the poet
Vivien Locke-Ellis in Selsfield.

In October Katherine again took LM with her to Paris, and on to
the Gurdjieff Institute for Harmonious Development, founded
upon Ouspensky's teachings, before sending her away. This community of well-intentioned people built her a little balcony where
the cows were kept so that she could inhale their 'curative vapours'.

Meanwhile, the young Murry, in his anguish at Katherine's
rejection of him, was intent on his own cure, his own purification.
Some thirty years later, in November 1951, he was to recall in his
Journal how he felt at the time:

> The Times says it was the driest October since 1922. For a
> wonder I could remember it clearly. It was the autumn I spent
> at Selsfield while K. was at Fontainebleau. And I remember
> particularly the dryness of the old sandstone quarry where I
> worked. I remember too that deadly feeling of desolation and
> emptiness, of our having drifted apart by some malign destiny,
> of her having gone where I could not follow, of the extreme
> agony of love when there is nothing to say.

* Katherine Mansfield to Samuel Koteliansky, 23rd August, 1922. Manuscript, British Museum.
† Manuscript, 1936.

Abandoning sessions of Yoga as being 'too contrived', his suffering and isolation even led him to attend a séance of tumbler-turning with two friends. He sat apart from them behind a screen as they laid their fingers on the glass, and framed his question in thought alone.

I put the only question which truly concerned me: 'What shall I do to be saved?' I don't think I put the question in that articulate form. As I remember it I simply asked: 'What shall I do?' Then rather slowly but completely without hesitation a strange answer was spelt out before my eyes. The answer was: 'Christ's Coat.' The meaning of the answer, or part of its meaning, was quickly clear to me. Christ's 'coat without a seam'—the vesture which was not parted among the soldiers, but for which they cast lots—has a hallowed place in Christian tradition. The interpretation seemed at the time obvious to me: I must become whole. It told me indeed nothing I did not know in some sense already: But it unlocked the knowledge from its dumb cradle—and set it before my imagination with a vividness that was almost terrifying.*

For twenty years he carried those two words with him in his wallet, just as they had been spelt out.

Katherine, convinced, after a few months at the Institute, that her treatment had been successful, asked him to join her for the New Year celebrations. Radiant with happiness as she showed him round the community and introduced him to the inmates, she told him how she had forced herself to leave him because they were killing each other. But now, purified and spiritually enriched, she was coming back to him. Together they would take a house in the country . . .

Her death in the evening of that same day has been told many times. Its mark upon her young husband when, with the blood pouring from her mouth, she looked at him with anguished, imploring eyes, while he was pushed out of the room by the doctors, was to last as long as his life.

His return to England after the funeral, when nothing

* Article in the magazine *The Aryan Path*, January 1938.

and nobody about him seemed to have any meaning or reality, and how, escaping from the many ladies only too eager to console him and 'replace' Katherine, he took his motorbike and alone rode out of London to a cottage he had been lent in Sussex near Ashdown Forest, has been told less often. Yet it is important, if we are to understand how the myth of Katherine Mansfield was created.

Aware that he had gone there for a purpose, yet unable to explain to himself what that purpose was, he sat on into the evening before the fire and forced himself to *face his aloneness*. When, every time, in fear, he wanted to turn away, he made himself face it again. It was then that he underwent one of the two crucial mystical experiences of his life. Many years later* he described it as a 'great liberation —not from her (Katherine), God knows: the absolute contrary —but a strange and enduring liberation from my Self. I surrendered, finally, to something. Call it a power, call it Life, call it Destiny, call it even God: but surrender I did, and I was purged of my Self. I became, in my meaning of the phrase, a religious man.'

This experience he always found very difficult to describe. By instinct he forced his frightened conscious Self into every part of his body until he felt he *was* in his hands and feet, as if he were a little island against whose slender shores a cold, dark, boundless ocean lapped devouring. 'Then a moment came when the darkness of the ocean changed to light, the cold to warmth . . . when it bathed me and I was renewed, when the room was filled with a presence and I knew I was not alone—that I never could be alone any more, that the universe held no menace for I was part of it, that I *belonged* . . . and because I belonged . . . I could never be afraid in the old ways or cowardly with the old cowardice.'†

He was to realise thereafter, he said later, that to love was more important than being loved.

Katherine would live on by the very fact of his own living love for her. He would not let her die. Her presence would accompany him always.

The altar was now draped for the Katherine Mansfield cult; the French threw themelves into it with even greater gusto than the

* Journal, 1955.
† *God*, 1929 (Cape), p. 36.

English. About my own youthful nostrils floated the perfumed incense of genius, sweet and sickly, indescribable, unnamable, invisible, and yet for ever there.

3

The Making of a Myth

About Katherine Mansfield's literary gifts my father had never had any doubts. As early as 1911, when he was editor of *Rhythm*,* he had recognised them, even before he had met her. As far as her personal life was concerned she concealed a great deal from him.

So he had an inspired vision of her, as near-perfect in genius as she had been as a woman. There was also the fact of his own deprived childhood, deprivation being the arch-creator of dreams.

Their youthful passion, made all the more real to us through its strains and stresses, with their quarrels and separations and reconciliations, was the attraction of opposites, even to their childhood backgrounds.

Katherine's was bright, carefree, comfortable and wealthy; surrounded by her sisters and brother, by her father, mother, grandmother, aunts and so forth—a vast family—in a New Zealand where the pioneering spirit and all that it brought with it of satisfaction and confidence, vitality and authority, was to set the whole pattern for her writing and her living.

How different his own.

He told me once that, as a small boy, in order to seek his mother's pardon for some offence, he slipped out of the house and spent all his savings on a bundle of kindling sticks for her, which he then proceeded to pop, one by one, through the letter-box. Perhaps, at that very hour, Katherine in New Zealand was on her grandmother's knee or playing hide-and-seek in the big garden at Karori.

In one of his novels my father wrote revealingly:

---

* A monthly literary magazine, 1911–1913 (which later became *The Blue Review*).

Now he came to think of it there was no sunlight in his memory at all. There was only gloom and grit and sordidness, amid which he had run like a drop of water in grey dust, complete and separate and hidden. And everything had been so huge, as though he was condemned to wander from cavern to cavern. Caverns and darkness and terrors! Oh yes, he had been loved by his mother and he had loved her. But somehow it had made no difference; it had never lighted the darkness or driven the terror away. Why did he always see her, as he saw her now, in an ugly grey cloth cap of his father's stuck through with an evil-looking hat pin, her hair looped untidily under it, her arms pink with soap and water, pegging out washing in a dark and mildewed garden? Why was the clasp of her fingers always soft and slimy with soapsuds, and the balls of her fingers so puckered and rough that he shrank under the touch? Why had there been no relief from it all, not one lovely, calm, sunlit thing to look back upon? Why had he worked with terror in his soul at his grammar school when he had taken his scholarship? Why had he never a moment's enjoyment of his own cleverness, even? Terror and darkness, terror and darkness . . .*

Of that particular darkness I saw the shade when, as a little girl, I and my brother, Col, stayed with our grandparents in their small terrace house in Brighton whither they had retired. I remember the dark, thick cloth on the table, the dark Victorian furniture, the sunless rooms with no flowers. My brother may have tasted something of the terror as he was 'assisted' down the garden path and sent flying through the gate with a vigorous kick in the backside from Granpa Murry who abhorred cheeky small boys. But as we went down to the sea, gaily swinging our painted tin buckets and wooden spades—my brother must have been about six and I seven at the time—our insouciance was still intact. My father, determined not to deprive his own children of the childhood that had been denied him, influenced perhaps by Katherine's, and certainly by Lawrence's precepts, left us free from too many constraints and too early a schooling.

We were spared the grind my father had known when he was

---

* *The Things We Are*, 1922 (Constable), p. 227.

made to pull and strain like a little pit-pony out of the poverty-trap, in the days when poverty was a deadly menace and his mother dared not call a doctor for fear of the expense; spared the stern parental will to success when, after his day as clerk at Somerset House his father, who worked every evening until midnight for 6d. an hour at the Penny Bank, would proudly perch his small son, scarcely three years old, upon a stool to read aloud from *The Times*.

The little prodigy was to obtain at his board school one of the six scholarships in the country for elementary school boys which took him to Christ's Hospital. There, at the Blue-coat school, he began his education in the Classics and became a Grecian. Then he won another scholarship, to Oxford, where, terrified lest anyone should discover his origins he pursued his classical studies with a kindly tutor who pinned high hopes on his brilliant pupil's future . . .

It takes no extreme effort of the imagination to understand the price he paid for this perpetual struggle.

Haunted by poverty and insecurity, his natural instincts for normal youthful activities became smothered beneath his prematurely developed intellect. The sheer effort to maintain his own integrity while he kept afloat in a society which was structured in those days only for the rich and privileged, robbed him of a carefree spontaneity. His highly sensitive nature grew inwards rather than outwards; contact with other human beings he found difficult. (Perhaps that was why he became such an outstanding literary critic: he discovered some of his deepest friendships in the minds of great writers and great men.)

So when my father fell in love with Katherine it was as with a rare, exotic, spoilt and beautiful bird, far, how far, from the kitchen sink. His own feathers seemed to him dull indeed. In an early novel* he created a heroine, plainly modelled on Katherine, who floats across the pages, superior, condescending, lovely, untouchable, 'tired of asking first-rate questions from second-rate people'. (The novels are, in general, a rich source of information about my father's life with Katherine Mansfield and the nature of their relationship.)

Even in the last novel he was to publish before abandoning the genre altogether, his main character, Wickham, who is in love with

---

* *Still Life*, 1916 (Constable).

Anne, is a 'queer fish', a 'man diseased whereas life was with Anne'.*

This 'queer fish' endured a lot from Katherine. One can almost hear her stern, schoolmistressy cross-questions when, in 1920, at the Villa Isola Bella on the Riviera, she challenged him over an innocent enough 'affair' with Princess Elizabeth Bibesco.

He was editing *The Athenaeum* in London at the time and had met Elizabeth, the daughter of Margot Asquith, at The Wharfe, the country seat of the Asquiths. His fondness for her was indubitably returned although it never went beyond an occasional embrace. Years later (in 1937) he was to meet her again and be deeply delighted.

In the winter he took time off from his office and went out to join Katherine who was very depressed. Elizabeth wrote to him in France. Katherine read the letters. In jealous anger she insisted that he send Elizabeth cold, formal replies. Katherine was seriously ill and he therefore complied, although he resented having to behave so brutally towards Elizabeth and loaded guilt upon himself:

> On this day Tig found me out in three lies about Elizabeth Bibesco.
>
> I felt a kind of numbed despair about myself. My being seemed to be split up, and unknown. There is the thing that lied; there was something unalterably true: the thing that played Tig false; the thing that is utterly loyal to her. By what right do I say the loyal part is more truly me than the other?
>
> I can see no right, yet I *know* it is true. I know it is true that I have not played her false with Elizabeth Bibesco, that the image of K. has always been present between me and E.B. as a flaming sword. And yet I lied.†

Katherine finally wrote to Elizabeth herself:

24.03.1921

Dear Princess Bibesco,

I am afraid you must stop writing these little love letters to my husband while he and I live together. It is one of the things which is not done in our world.

* *The Voyage,* 1924 (Constable).

† Entry in manuscript notebook dated 'Isola Bella, Wednesday, June 5th, 1920'.

You are very young. Won't you ask your husband to explain to you the impossibility of such a situation.

Please do not make me have to write to you again. I do not like scolding people and I simply hate having to teach them manners.

Yours sincerely,

Katherine Mansfield*

One would think he had *slept* with Elizabeth Bibesco! Which he had not. One wonders at Katherine's harshness in the light of the fact that her ailments were due to her own past promiscuities as well as consumption, and that five years previously she had gone off with Francis Carco. The complete freedom Murry gave Katherine *because* he loved her, she was far from allowing him. That my father desperately needed affection, and that there were women in plenty ready to supply it, made it all the more surprising that he was so faithful to Katherine.

But they were young, and this must never be forgotten. That the love of Murry and Katherine was unattainable in its completeness; that his longing for 'a cheap ordinary happiness at 6¾d. a yard' with her was always to be denied him, did not alter the fact that it was entirely genuine, no spurious imitation or intellectual idea.

It was the love of these two outsiders for one another that was to bear its own unique and strange fruit as the inspiration of much of my father's life in after years. Her love for him finds one of its many utterances in a letter she wrote for him in Switzerland and entrusted to the bank until after her death:

Dearest Bogey,

I have been on the point of writing this letter for days. My heart has been behaving in such a curious fashion that I can't imagine it means nothing. So, as I should hate to leave you unprepared, I'll just try and jot down what comes into my mind. All my manuscripts I leave entirely to you to do what you like with. Go through them one day, dear love, and destroy all

* Typed copy of letter in the Humanities Research Center, University of Texas, Austin, Texas. Quoted by Antony Alpers in *The Life of Katherine Mansfield*, 1980 (Viking Press).

you do not use. Please destroy all letters you do not wish to keep and all papers. You know my love of tidiness. Have a clean sweep, Bogey, and leave all fair—will you?

Books are yours of course ... Monies, of course, are all yours. In fact, my dearest dear, I leave everything to you—to the secret you whose lips I kissed this morning. In spite of everything—how happy we have been! I feel no other lovers have walked the earth more joyfully—in spite of all.

> Farewell—my precious love
> I am for ever and ever
>
> Your
>
> WIG

And his for her when he wrote in his Journal in 1950:

I am reading the proofs of Katherine's letters ... to read them is the same old agony. I have to steel myself to go on. And then suddenly it seems all strange, and I ask myself: 'Did this really happen once to her and to me? Where and what is this "me" to whom it happened?' And then I ask myself: 'Have I kept faith with my darling?' And I feel deep in my soul a great joy, because I know that I have. And then I feel strangely that I am in touch with her. I don't know what this feeling *means*: whether that she lives in me, or lives in some other place, or something else, for ever unutterable. But it is as though she gazed into my soul—my old, weather-beaten soul—and smiled and gave it her blessing, and said: 'You *have* been faithful to what we gave each other, to what we learned, to what we were: and I am for ever and for ever your Wig.' But darling, you know as well as I that it was no merit in me. Something grew up between us to which I could not but be faithful—to have betrayed it was beyond my power, because I should have ceased to *be*. The bitterest years were those in which it and I had to struggle with the wild beast, and it saved me.

It was, however, a strange and unreal Katherine, now dead, whom he placed beside all his other dead heroes who were so much nearer to him than most of his living contemporaries; those heroes of the past, the young and the lovely and the pure in heart—Christ, Chekhov, Keats. 'I have lived by Keats' truth,' he was to write before he died, 'the marvel of Johnnie Keats five foot high.'* And Katherine he would present to the public, he would reveal her genius, aye, *give* her to the public and then stand aside.

There were difficulties. How could he apply to his own beloved dead wife the full force of his critical abilities which demanded the painstaking research he lavished on John Keats and Fanny Brawne, for instance? How could he probe into her past which she had, so evidently, wanted to destroy and forget? No, he could not bring himself to do this inhuman thing. Love and loyalty came before literature. Let the students who came after him rake up what they must.

* Journal, 1955.

4

Violet

'It was in her eyes . . . I am not a dabbler in the occult, in fact I keep away from the stuff, I don't like it. BUT I am convinced that Katherine possessed your mother. You see, Katherine did *not* want to die . . . I saw her when she was only a skeleton but the expression in her eyes was indubitably of someone who did not want to go.'

My uncle, Richard Murry, told me this in the summer of 1980. I listened to him in silence. He laid aside the jumper he had been darning with the apple he had held into the hole. Across his very blue, piercing eyes passed a shadow, as if he were watching the life of his brother, my father, unfold itself once more. The white roses tangling in the branches of the old apple tree trailed down to the grass in clusters. On a tree trunk beside him glowed the sun of the Loire Valley imprisoned in a bottle of Rosé d'Anjou, the small luxury he had brought on his holiday with me.

'Why,' he went on, 'your mother's very handwriting became so identical with Katherine's that neither your father, nor Margaret Scott,* nor Alpers recognised that a letter of hers describing Sister Verity was not one of Katherine's describing LM!'

I remembered Sister Verity, my mother's nurse with her coal-black eyes, who kept a switch behind the door to beat Col and me when we were naughty, but I still said nothing.

However, at a later date I was astonished to find an entry of my mother's in the front page of Chekhov's *The Darling*:

Bought on a day of most wonderful elation. Mr Middleton Murry has been talking with me about my work. He says I

---

* Margaret Scott had transcribed the early Mansfield manuscripts in the Turnbull Library in New Zealand.

show the most *amazing* promise and that he was astounded.
He is going to print some of my stuff . . .

This was written on 25th October, 1923. She could not at that
date have been familiar with Katherine's handwriting and yet the
likeness is remarkable.

Reluctant to press my uncle over a past tragedy to which he had
been very close, I was only the more aware that the ghost of
Katherine would not be still. What do you want with me? I
challenged her silently. Why won't you die in a decent, ordinary
fashion? Why do you pull at my heart-strings so? Why will you not
let me go as my young mother did?

On my father, who had buried Katherine Mansfield at Fontainebleau in January 1923, the influence of her restless ghost was
incalculable: she became an integral part of his living. His friends
and acquaintances failed to understand this, for outwardly he
seemed scarcely to mourn her and they were shocked as, quite
indifferent to social convention, he continued his life, apparently
unaffected.

*   *   *

It was in the autumn of 1923 that he first met Violet le Maistre, a
young woman who brought her writing for him to criticise. Discern-
ing 'the authentic note' of the same order as Katherine Mansfield's,
he suggested that she read Chekhov of whom she had never heard.*
Then he found himself thinking that this pretty and talented girl
really ought to be kept in the family; she was the very girl for his
brother Richard, thirteen years younger than himself.

He lent Violet his Constance Garnett translations of Chekhov's
short stories, introduced her to his artist brother and invited her to
supper.

In his London flat, on the evening he expected her, he was
preparing *filet mignon* and had some of his brother's work ready to
show her. She was late. Anxiously he went again and again to the
window. When at last she did arrive, flushed and wind-blown, she
explained breathlessly that she had planned to be on the tick of time
but had lost the way.

When the meal was over he enthusiastically produced Richard's
sketches. But suddenly he heard her saying in her low voice:

* Manuscript, 1936.

'Mr Murry, I like these drawings, and I like your brother very much; but I can't love him because, you see, it is *you* whom I love.'

The loveliness of this young creature whose dark eyes sparkled with a living gaiety that seemed to have passed out of his life years ago,* touched a chord in his heart. He muttered that he was too old for her, but she brushed that aside, saying:

'The only question is: Do you love me?'

'I didn't know I did; but I do,' he answered and he took her in his arms, amazed, 'so old and battered', at being thus loved by one so young.†

'Probably I couldn't love anyone but a girl,' he was to confide to his Journal some years later.‡ 'I don't know what Woman is: and never shall. Not that I have avoided Woman. It is simply that I can't see, can't make contact with Woman. She doesn't exist for me. A sort of Bogy of whom I hear report. Not in my destiny . . .'

Violet was indeed only a girl. No more than twenty-three when my father married her, she had led a sheltered existence in select boarding schools and a college of dramatic art. An early photograph of her peeping out from her mother's skirts, laughing, speaks from the sepia of smocks and lace of a cherished mother–daughter love in a sunny, tasteful and privileged home.

At their engagement my father gave her the little pearl ring he had once given to Katherine. Then, breathing a happiness that had been so long absent from his life, he took a holiday with his brother Richard in Dorset and relinquished his motorbike for his first car, a Model T Ford, 'the old Trojan' as we were to call it. It was then, as they were swimming off the Chesil Beach, that he saw, lying low facing the sea, isolated, half-hidden in its tamarisks, the timber-clad, white-painted Old Coastguard Station. By chance or destiny, passing through Dorchester on their way back from their holiday, they saw that this very dream house was up for sale by auction. Not knowing where the money was coming from, rashly he bid for it and acquired it. Again by chance or destiny a cheque for £1,000 royalties on Katherine's books, far more than she had ever received during her life-time, arrived for him a day later. The gods were smiling. The house was his. The herons of his and Katherine's

* Since 1917 when the doctor had diagnosed Katherine's fatal illness.
† This whole scene is recorded in a manuscript of 1947.
‡ Journal, 30th October, 1930.

dream farm had transformed themselves into swans that honked as they flew over the roof-top from the swannery while the waves pounded on the pebble shore.

So it was to the Old Coastguard Station that he took his girl-wife in that summer of 1924, with his books and papers and the few items of furniture and ornaments he had collected with Katherine. They engaged a gardener and a housekeeper, arranged for his friends, the Tomlinsons,* to occupy part of the house, planted fruit trees, dug the garden, painted and repaired the house, with Richard coming to help at weekends.

Violet went on writing short stories. They were published over the name of Mary Arden which my father chose for her. He was invited to deliver the Clark Lectures at Cambridge, which he afterwards developed into *Keats and Shakespeare*, published in 1925. For him it was like the golden days of the Villa Pauline all over again.

But after some months he noticed that Violet's gaiety had disappeared. At first he thought it was only a malaise due to her first pregnancy. One day, however, she said that she had a confession to make that might hurt him. But what could hurt him, he reassured her, when he loved her so much? 'Golly,' she said (that was her name for him with his black curly hair, after a golliwog she had loved as a little girl), 'Golly, I don't really want this baby. I've tried to want it but I can't. I only want you. I'm afraid it will come between us. You won't love me so much. You will love her—I know you will.'†

He was indeed deeply shocked. I do not think he ever understood Violet in this. A young woman must have absolute security in love before she can willingly make herself a nest for children; it was something Violet needed time for. She knew she had somehow been cheated of it and that nothing could ever now give her the freedom of loving and growing with the man she loved. As for my father, had he but realised it, although he loved Violet dearly he was still immersed in Katherine.

So, while he reassured her that a child would only unite them the more, Violet knew that this could not be. Violet was not Katherine

* H. M. Tomlinson, the novelist.
† Manuscript, 1947.

and had not Katherine's experience. Her innocence was real, whereas Katherine's had been make-believe.

The little girl my father and Katherine had longed for was born to Violet. And, as she had predicted, it came between them. Violet turned away from the baby and it could not thrive. Determined to save it, my father took it up from its bed of newspapers and searched and searched for the right food with which he fed it from a silver porringer.

This is how I struggled into life.

To the sound of the Atlantic breakers my father went on with his writing, while Katherine's 'presence' pervaded everything: her possessions were all about the house, not a memorabilia to be hallowed, but just part of the household scene that he thought no more of discarding or putting away than a snail would its shell. As he cared for me and I began to grow strong, an indissoluble bond was created, a tie with his world not only of the present but of the past, too, a world that was like a fluid, part of and yet distinct from our day-to-day living, something which we both knew of yet never spoke about.

It was not be wondered that my mother felt lost. Deeply in love with my father, she must have found in this most kind and loving man an elusive *je ne sais quoi*, a preoccupation with worlds she could not enter, that no living soul could penetrate.

How grey the waves must have seemed to Violet as they crashed onto the Chesil Beach beyond the windows, greyer than they had been even to her forefathers in their rowing boat when they escaped from France and the Huguenot persecutions, to the island of Jersey.

And then a strange thing happened. She cut her chestnut curls and combed her hair straight with a fringe across her brow in Katherine's style. I doubt whether my father even noticed—he had a way of simply not noticing.

He did notice, however, that a shadow had fallen between them in his fight for the baby's life.

It was at this time that Lawrence returned from New Mexico, disenchanted with America. He and my father had a friendly meeting in London in October 1925. He had apparently forgiven my father for not having gone with him to New Mexico and promised to visit the Old Coastguard Station with Frieda. According to my father he seemed much gentler. He said he was going to settle in northern Italy and my father promised that if he did so, he and Violet would go out there to stay with him and Frieda.

However, by the time they were to go, Violet was pregnant again. My father did not want to risk the long journey with her to Spotorno, carrying a six months' baby, and refused to leave her behind. Lawrence was furious. Once again my father had let him down; once again he had put his wife first. My father found him unfair. Their friendship was again severely shaken and my father, although reasoning that if this was Lawrence's friendship he would have none of it, grieved in his heart.*

In May 1926 my brother was born. 'Another John Middleton, ye gods!' wrote Lawrence to Koteliansky.†

*   *   *

Soon afterwards, weakened by successive pregnancies, Violet fell seriously ill. My father's life-long friend, Dr James Carruthers Young, who had been at the Gurdjieff Institute when Katherine had died and was to come and live near us at Larling, diagnosed pulmonary tuberculosis.

Could she have been saved? Certainly, if it had depended upon my father's love and care alone. He resolved to fight this deadly disease. This time, if it had to be a sanatorium, then so be it. He would not make the same mistake as with Katherine and shrink from taking all the steps necessary for a cure. He summoned the courage to tell Violet the truth but was completely unprepared for her reply:

'Oh, I'm so *glad*!' she said. 'I wanted this to happen.'

'You wanted this to happen,' he repeated slowly and dully as his world turned upside down and he stared into her shining eyes.

'You see, Golly,' she explained, 'I wanted you to love me as much as you loved Katherine—and how could you, without this?'‡

He did all he could to reason her out of her absurd, childish doubts, the terrible result of his immersion in Katherine. But no amount of sensible argument on his part could persuade Violet that she must not succumb. She said she agreed but in fact she had fallen in love with death, that tragic death of the young and beautiful, that

---

* *Reminiscences of D. H. Lawrence*, 1933 (Cape).
† D. H. Lawrence to Samuel Koteliansky, 28th June, 1926.
‡ Manuscript, 1947.

spoke to my father in his deepest being and, in his mystic contempla-
tion of it, did so much to create the myth of Katherine Mansfield.

'There was death in her face,' wrote Mrs Thomas Hardy, one day
when she had been to visit us, 'she looked so pretty.'*

During the ensuing years, while my brother and I were growing
up, my father resolutely put Violet in a sanatorium, but to no avail.
He finally gave up our beautiful Dorset home and bought South
Acre, a spacious bungalow nearer to London, at Yateley in Hampshire, where she could be more easily looked after. Distracted with
grief, he found himself quite unable to communicate with anyone
and 'stewed in the juice of his own agony'.†

One evening at the bungalow he wrote:

> At 10 o'clock Violet called me in. She said, 'You won't be
> cross because I called you, Golly?' It's an aching bruise to think
> there have been times when I have been cross: but there it is.
> 'Did Wingfield say anything about my chest?'
>
> 'He said it was the old cavity causing the sputum.'
>
> 'That's a good thing, isn't it? I don't mind about that. I know
> it's all rotten up there. What would be awful would be if the
> good part were getting active.'
>
> 'Yes, that would be bad. He says that as soon as the
> temperature goes down, he's going on with the Sanaskrisin.'
>
> 'Yes, he told me that.'
>
> 'How beautiful your little lamp is,' I said. 'It has a little halo.'
> It looked lovely, and so peaceful, as I sat facing it on the bed,
> and she looked lovely and happy. There had just been a tremor
> of fear when she asked: 'Did Wingfield say anything about my
> chest?' but it was light, like a thistledown blown away. Now
> she was happy, with me there, holding her hand.
>
> 'It makes just the right light,' she said.
>
> Oh my sweetheart! Sweetheart—that is the only word. Oh,
> you who come after me, don't let a woman become your
> sweetheart. It's unbearable—unbearable: just unbearable. For
> she will die, and the world will stand still, and your heart will
> burst. I have had two sweethearts.

* *The Personal Notebooks of Thomas Hardy*, ed. Richard H. Taylor, 1979
(Macmillan), p. 286.
† Journal, 2nd November, 1951.

And my heart is breaking again, but oh more terribly.

Katherine had her life, but Violet has had nothing—nothing: and I have known the end from the beginning. But when the end comes, you know only that you haven't known it, that you can't know it. It is all new, all unbearable.

There is *nothing* to save you—nothing at all.

Why should *you* be saved? Of course, you don't want to be saved. If I could die now, this instant, I would refuse.

I must be there, quiet and calm, to the end: to *help*, to love, to help by being there to be loved. Then, afterwards, to die.

Oh help me, Powers, to help—to be stronger than my love, to ignore the anguish. To be *strong*. To be *strong*. To BE STRONG.*

And then, as Katherine had left him to go to Fontainebleau, so Violet left him to go to a great friend of his, Max Plowman and his wife Dorothy. They felt they could save her: through their devotion to her they would give her the will to live and prove the healing power of love. He no more believed it than he had Gurdjieff's teachings. However, they moved her to their house in London. A few months later, in their 'cloudy room' as she called it, she died ecstatically happy, just as Katherine had been at the end of her life.

It is small wonder that my father saw in his destiny at that time 'only Love, and the inevitable disaster of Love'.†

Not only was it the disaster of Love but the disaster of the myth of youthful love and its innocence. 'We were playing at man and wife,' he wrote many years later, 'and the game had turned dreadful. The child-wife greeted with ecstasy this romantic disease.'‡

Violet's innocence was only equalled, perhaps surpassed, by his own, although he was fourteen years her senior. He never even realised that she had died of love for him. While he poured his life and soul and much of his vitality into his books, absent on his long voyages of the mind, Violet's youthful gaiety and vivacity faded ineluctably into melancholy. Without Katherine's physical and psychological need for another woman alongside her husband, without therefore an 'LM' to turn to, Violet's life was over almost before it had begun.

* Journal, 2nd December, 1930.
† Journal, 30th October, 1930.
‡ Manuscript, 1947.

5

The 'Earth-woman'

During the last years of my mother's life at Yateley my father had difficulties with his household: friends noticed that he was neglected: his jackets were frayed and the buttons not sewn on; one of my mother's nurses turned out to be a drunkard, another slothful. With the exception of our nanny nothing seemed to be as it should.

So in May 1930 the nurses were dismissed and a certain Ada Elizabeth Cockbayne, a farmer's daughter from Northampton-shire, was engaged as housekeeper. She was in her thirties and an excellent cook. Nothing else was known about her and my father asked nothing.

Tall, fair, sturdy, good-looking and capable, she was anything but an intellectual. Books were only things to be banged together to get the dust out. But then domestic duties were all that were required of her, and as she busied herself putting order in the house she would make my mother's laughter ring out when she came into her room in the morning, poker in hand, to 'bugger the fire'.

What a treasure! My father could sigh with relief that he was free now to work in peace; he was even able to go to the South of France to attend the funeral of Lawrence, the man who had so loved and so reviled him. There he met Frieda again and it is odd to think that she could have become my stepmother . . .

Many years later she was to tell him that his 'gentlemanly' behaviour with her on their journey to Germany in 1923 had averted an ugly tragedy.

In my father's last novel, which he gave to Violet, he put into the mouth of his hero these strangely prophetic words:

I thought you might be diabolically clever and determined and cruel. And that fascinated me. I should like to be destroyed by someone, some woman, you know. Really annihilated. The moth in the candle-flame.*

And Frieda was not a destroyer.

It was as if the Great War, in which nearly all his Oxford contemporaries had been killed, held its horror in reserve for him to live through in his private life, this strange man who strongly attracted people and yet did not want to be known, who found human contacts so difficult and yet whom no woman ever refused.

He did not want to be known, had never wanted to *know* Katherine Mansfield. To be trusted and loved, yes, as he would love and trust, but not to be *known*. In 1954, on reading Iris Murdoch's novel *Under the Net*, he wrote in his Journal of

a false idea of the knowledge of persons. Indeed it is true one never *knows* them, but this is no tragedy as, for example, Tom Eliot represents it to be. It would be a terrible thing if one did *know* them. It would result in a petrification of human relations. It is a false ideal and a false tragedy. What one seeks is not to know a human being but to trust him or her. And that is not 'simply a kind of co-existence'—Eliot's Edward and Lavinia —but veritably a new and blessed relation, which is to me the only relation worthy of the name of love.

When in 1953 some facts about Katherine's private life were forced upon my father by Antony Alpers' first biography of her,† it did not matter greatly to him. And this leads me to think that had he been alive to read that biographer's later complete study, it would have concerned him little more. That the person he loved was 'eaten hollow with selfishness', as one critic described Katherine, did not seem to make any impression on my father at all. It was the fact of love itself, the love-relationship, that mattered—the myth of the loved one. Whatever sins had been brought to light by students of Katherine's life, her myth would have remained intact as far as my father was concerned.

In 1954 he was to write in his Journal:

* *The Voyage*, 1924 (Constable).
† Antony Alpers, *Katherine Mansfield: A Biography*, 1954 (Cape).

. . . in so far as I did contribute to the 'legend', I did it in all innocence. I knew nothing of Katherine's past. She did not tell me about it; she did not want to tell me; she wanted to forget and obliterate it. And I forbore to enquire. Love is trust. And unless she were to have spoken freely, of her own motion, it was not for me to pry. (That I *now* think she might have been happier if I had asked her to tell me is beside the point.)

I suppose people will find it hard to believe that I was what I was: that, for instance, in spite of all the evidence, I did not believe she intended to be Carco's lover in February 1916. It is true I should not have attempted to restrain her, if she had told me outright; because I believed, as I believe today, that Love is free. If she wanted to go to Carco, that was that: I would not utter a word to restrain her. It was for her to decide. Oh, she would have liked it better (I have no doubt) if I had not left her absolutely free—if I had made a scene. But, deep down, I was absolutely certain that she would return to me. And because of that deep faith in the enduringness of our love, I did not face in imagination her determination to be his lover: that was unreal to me, as (in a slightly different sense) it proved to be unreal to her. I did not believe it, or in it. And I was right.

Thus, in a way involuntarily, I presented the essential Katherine which, some will say, is, by comparison with the real Katherine, legendary. She had to struggle—and sometimes she ought to have struggled harder than she did—to eliminate the impurities, the residues from herself. But her struggle was a noble one . . .

I have no regrets. Our love was Love. If we failed each other, we knew we had failed, and returned to our reality, as a compass-needle to the pole. But the truth about us—that will have to wait for *many* years.

But obviously my father in 1954 was not the same man as in 1927, when he tried in vain to argue Violet out of her death-wish. Perhaps he could not explain to his girl-wife that knowing her was for him a form of possession which he rejected to 'let the loved one be'. Thus the dead Katherine could remain intact, untroubled by obscene knowing, but Violet would pine in the loneliness of not being known.

*   *   *

After my mother's death in March 1931, my grieving father turned once more to *Fantasia of the Unconscious*. Had he not, he wondered, loved Violet and Katherine from what Lawrence, in his book, called the 'upper centres' which 'led to phthisis'? 'Woman is really polarised downwards, towards the centre of the earth ...' Lawrence went on, '... her deepest consciousness is in the loins and belly. Pervert this and you get a race of "intelligent women" who then become perverse.'* Could Lawrence perhaps be right?

There was Miss Cockbayne, she attracted him, my father told himself, and he certainly did not love her from 'the upper centres'. She was fond of him, the children liked her and in running the house she was proving invaluable.

The more he thought of it the more he convinced himself that Lawrence must be right: the answer to the future lay on his very doorstep. He would ask Miss Cockbayne to marry him.

Friends threw up their hands in horror and dismay. What could he possibly have in common with her? Violet was scarcely cold in her grave. Miss Cockbayne's sisters wrote and warned him that their sister had an uncontrollable temper ...

But, spiritually exhausted and physically deprived, he was deaf to entreaties. Mildly he said that he did not expect it to be 'all plain sailing' and then married Miss Cockbayne, or Betty as we now called her, at Odiham Registry Office, two months after the death of Violet.

Thus was my father impelled into such a mis-match as to make Tolstoy's marriage with Sonia Behrs appear very heaven by comparison.

My mother's portrait he hung up in his study beside that of Katherine. 'I have learnt what few men have ever learnt about life from these two lovely women,' he wrote in his Journal.† These things he buried deep in his soul. Bent on a goal that no one understood, deaf to all entreaties, he pursued his course towards a living hell.

It is more than likely that Betty herself feared the miseries that were in store for them both if they remained together. For, one day

---

* D. H. Lawrence, *Fantasia of the Unconscious*, 1923 (*The Adelphi*); 1930 (Martin Secker).

† Journal, 12th April, 1931.

in 1931, after we had moved to Larling in Norfolk, her baby still
unborn, she set off for the station in tears. When my father found
her she begged him to let her go away, only giving her a little money
to bring up the child herself so that it would never know him.
Amazed and mystified, he persuaded her to return. Was not the
baby his as well? During their later rows she would reproach him
bitterly. 'Why couldn't you have let me go? I had all I wanted: your
baby; why did you make me come back?' Then she would cry,
'You're a fool—a fool. Don't you know that women are all
bitches—all of them!'*

The disaster Betty had foreseen inexorably took place. The
marriage that he had told Max Plowman would 'not be all plain
sailing' turned out to be a wreck of appalling dimensions. There was
no common ground between Betty and himself at all. In abandoned
fits of temper and unbridled jealousies, quite unable to understand
my father's withdrawn and deeply tender nature, poor Betty, a
victim of her own primal emotions, was to goad and torture him
ceaselessly into the sheer animality of *knowing* her. The very
annihilation he had once prophesied as desirable, the 'destruction
by some woman', was to take him through the soul-destroying
degradations of their *réconciliations sur l'oreiller* for the next ten
years, until in 1941 his health and spirit were so far broken as to
take from him the very strength to remain with Betty and rear their
infant son, David; until, as he was to put it, 'gangrene in his soul had
turned to gangrene in his legs'.†

And yet, all through those terrible years, his love for Katherine
remained a constant reality, the world of not knowing but trusting,
and of fidelity in trust. 'One must *learn* to love,' he had said. He was
to learn that almost at the cost of his life. As for his children, the
effect of growing up in a constant atmosphere of terrifying, uncontrolled rages, was traumatic indeed.

* Manuscript, 1947.
† *Idem*, 1947.

PART II

ENACTMENT

1

My Earliest Days

As I write this, in a foreign country, I can see out of my window the cherry tree, its sticky buds waiting through the long cold of February and March, waiting to break out into leaf. Its bare boughs are black and stiff against the pale sky. They could be dead. Just as part of me seemed dead when I left England long ago, fleeing those 'sneaping winds at home' in search of what I knew not.

Wherever I journeyed I was pursued by the feeling that I did not, could not belong, but that once I had been part of some lost world that now I dared not fathom.

Abroad, I fell ill and tried to explain to a psychiatrist, a stranger and unacquainted with English literature, how, when I read in my father's autobiography his account of Katherine Mansfield's death, my grief was so unbearable that I could not bring myself to open the book again.

'That is natural,' said the doctor, 'since you are the daughter of your father's first marriage.'

'Oh no,' I corrected him, 'you misunderstand me. My mother was Violet le Maistre. My father married her sixteen months after his first wife's death. I was born the following year. She died when I was six.'

But the doctor was adamant. Out of politeness I argued no more, although I gave no credence to this strange statement of his and soon banished it from my mind.

Many years later—long after my father's death—I stumbled upon a note of his written after he had seen my baby son for the first time: 'I am as convinced as I am of anything important in this life that Katherine's spiritual heritage has been passed on. I always felt, quite simply, that Violet's daughter was Katherine's daughter and I named her accordingly. I loved my little daughter as Katherine would have loved her, with *her* love as well as my own . . .'

It was upon reading this that my past life and present aspirations became clear. The guilts that had been inbred in me by others' bitter jealousies, both silent and uttered, had debarred me from a vanished world. I vowed that none would tear it away from me again, this most precious spiritual heritage. Now it was up to me to go forward. I seized the golden thread.

My hesitant journey took me first to my father's Journals and then, in 1982, shyly, to Arthur and Cynthia Koestler's country cottage in Suffolk. Arthur was very ill but they received me with infinite warmth and kindness. We talked about a meeting he had had with my father, about the present book, and he asked me many questions. As we talked on I tried to sift in my mind the urgent from the non-urgent topics so as not to tire him with idle chatter. Then he said gently: 'Now tell me, Katherine, please, what do you want to ask me?'

And that which had weighed upon me for so long came to my lips:

'I would like to know what you think is the most important thing of all in this life.'

He pondered for a while and then said slowly, carefully:

'To be deeply attached to something, or someone perhaps. It is the *attachment* that counts.'

This great European, whose writing I had admired so much for so many years, had given me the answer I was seeking. No longer, I felt, was I only fit to crawl into a corner and die.

As he accompanied me to the gate the sunflowers stood like sentinels against his cottage walls. Noticing my appreciation he said: 'They remind me of Hungary, you see.'

Everything was bathed in an immense rosy flush from the setting sun.

'How beautiful this evening is,' he said as he seemed to breathe it in for eternity, surveying it all, the fields and the woods in peace, with his strange eyes, milky-blue . . .

I went away as if touched by magic, in silent praise of my heroes. For here was another brave man like my father, who had tested his beliefs upon the very fabric of life itself, without fear or favour, searching always for the truth.

So, finally, I turned to my own childhood memories, the precious moments and those that were painful to relive, able through my father's Journals to compare his impressions of specific events with my own, and to see the truth emerging. I found myself wondering at his nearness to me and, at the same time, his apparently contradictory remoteness. Often his writings seemed to have little connection with what was going on around him, but this was how things were. Once inside his study he was oblivious of the world outside his door.

'Don't you *sicken* of shutting that door and sitting down to that table?' Katherine Mansfield once wrote to him from Fontainebleau.*

But it did not sicken him at all. He was immersed in his countries of the mind; for as far back as I can remember this was so.

*   *   *

My earliest recollections are of the Old Coastguard Station and of the sea pounding frighteningly beyond our lawn that ran down to Chesil Beach. The shingles hard on the feet. A whole world stretching, surrounding infant consciousness, mysterious, sometimes terrifying, wildly wonderful, set even then with beauties: the sea-pinks bowing in the wind along the path that skirted the beach and led down to the house, the lawn itself. We were surrounded by the sea, hemmed in, protected yet menaced. The great guns from the warships far out in the grey distance filled me with terror, the foreboding of some awful catastrophe, as I clung to the bars of my cot. And in winter the sea lay silent in icy mists as I sat in the back of our car, the old Trojan, and watched my father puffing and blowing and swearing as, with immense efforts, he turned and turned the handle and the water was frozen in the radiator.

My pity was unspoken as I sat helpless in the back, waiting. Poor Dadda. He might kill himself groaning like that . . . My heart swelled.

The world was fraught with difficulties.

My mother was a shadow with a low voice, gentle, absent. She moved, a vague presence. I cannot ever remember her embracing me nor ever remember her laugh. A voice like the wind from the sea, she mingled with the elements, a spirit unpositive and lost. Had she ever

---

* Katherine Mansfield to John Middleton Murry, 12th November, 1922.

laughed? Did she ever look down on me in my barred cot? All I knew was that she was sad, that nothing could change that.

As for myself, I was called Katherine Violet. Not Violet Katherine. I was the 'egg-weg'. I was Weg.

The reality was my father. He suffered, laughed, cursed, shut himself up in his study, took me on his knee, helped me as I would help him—sponge his back in his bath, pick up his tools, hand him whatever he needed. He was Jove. In him was all power, all wisdom; his thunder was mighty, his tenderness manna. The only god. My mother brought me into the world. My father nurtured me, brought the ailing baby through to life and health and once turned me upside down and shook me when I had swallowed a plum stone.

Up the winding path where the sea-pinks blow and back again to our house, on the postman's back. Pig-a-back. My brother Col and I took turns. Raids to my father's study, to his desk where lay all the wonders of the world: pots of pens and pencils, feathers and pen-wipers, sealing wax, paper-clips, old nails, boxes of string and rubber bands, pins, drawing pins and even dates or sugared almonds or ginger. And, pervading all, the smell of books and tobacco and soap and tweed, that sweet smell of safety which was home.

Days of youngest childhood when my world, encompassed by that great ocean, was ruled by a benign tyrant: my father's comings and goings like those of the sun, the comfort of his knee the only one. Tyrant to be worshipped and sometimes attacked when the spirit of daring blazed, when Col and I were one tribe and grown-ups another, when we would bolt from his study with some treasure, our hearts fit to burst, and the blood racing through our veins like heady wine.

I was fat, wilful and not necessarily very nice, with boot-button eyes and a Cheshire Cat grin.

Occasionally we would visit Thomas Hardy and his wife, Florence, who were my god-parents and lived nearby. I can remember him sitting me on his knee and fashioning gently, with gnarled old hands that shook, a rabbit with his red-spotted handkerchief and waggling its ears with his fingers inside to make me laugh.

But my mother did not like the Old Coastguard Station. Its loneliness and isolation—that very isolation my father sought —rested heavily upon her.

When she fell ill and we left the sea for Hampshire, nothing was essentially changed for me: my father still shut himself in his study, my brother and I still played wild games, my uncle still came and painted his pictures, my mother still lay in bed and coughed. In a word, we were safe.

How could I know how brief that safety was to be, how fateful that cough? And when my father sat at his desk on an autumn evening, writing his Journal, he simply did not understand what had happened to Violet, beyond the grim reality of her illness.

October 30th, 1930. The book on Lawrence has been written—it was finished today.* It's six months since the last note was written. And during those six months, Violet has gone steadily downhill. Tonight, for the first time, I felt that she was really giving up hope. 'She didn't mind dying so much,' she said, 'though that was bitter enough, but she couldn't bear the thought of the pain it would be to me.' I lay there helpless and hopeless beside her, trying to be still inside. And I thought: Would it be such great pain to me? Yes, probably, pretty terrible. The bonds of love are ill to loose; and I love her. And the thing that is numb inside me, having struggled in vain, and watched her illness all these years, would wake to life and shriek for the pain. She is lovely, gentle, tender, gay, innocent, a creature made to love and be loved. Perhaps one day Weg or Col will read these words. And they will be sad and happy at once to think that their mother was a girl so adorable. Somehow, she has never been more than a girl . . .

I don't know, never shall know, why Love leads to this inevitable disaster. But it's manifest that I am incapable of anything else. Lawrence tried the other way, and ended by dreaming of that with which I began. The end of Lawrence's life is the beginning of mine. It's quite mysterious—utterly beyond my understanding. But there's some deep connection. Deny love, and it's disaster; accept it, and it's disaster.

Nanny put newspapers into her cast-off shoes to make them fit and, buttoning my brother and me into our brown gaiters, warning us not to jump in the puddles, she took us for afternoon walks

* *Son of Woman*, 1931 (Cape).

through the muddy lanes lined with tall trees whose branches sometimes met high over our heads. We picked blackberries and she made us blackberry and apple jam which she put into potted meat jars for us. We each had our own special pot. Sometimes she would frown at me. 'You are your father's favourite,' she would say, 'it's not fair.' She preferred little boys. At those moments it was as if an invisible dagger stabbed me under the ribs . . .

Col and I each had a child's golf club and were taken to the course with my father and James Carruthers Young who, my father said, 'blasphemed his way round'.

As in Dorset, we quite often visited our neighbours where, during afternoon tea, we once adorned my father with a garland of cotton reels which he wore all the way home.

It was at this time that he met Sir Richard Rees and Max Plowman. Max began to play a growing part not only in my father's life but in my mother's, too. She responded to his love for her, not unnaturally perhaps, by loving him. My father's feelings were mixed. He was indebted to Max for all his efforts to cure her but he did not want to lose her to him in the process.

She came back from the Midhurst Sanatorium no better than before and in the afternoons my father tried to bury his grief by digging and planting our garden. Once again his mind went back to the Rananim ideal:

December 10th, 1930. I found, to my joy, that Max also holds that man must take his rhythm from the earth. After lunch I had been talking, once more, to V. about the necessity of simplifying and becoming self-supporting, as far as possible, on the land. She said promptly:

> In spite of feet and fingers numb
> Back to the land we all must come.

I couldn't believe it was impromptu. She said there was no place for her in the new scheme. Is that true? If so, it must be changed. The scheme must be a scheme for a living V., not a dead one. It's hard, seeing what a jolt I have had, to reckon on her living. And yet I must. To do otherwise is to take life away from her.

But the fact that during this crisis the only real relief I have had has been in digging, preparing for growth, shows how profound in me this need of the earth is. It's elemental, and more elemental than the need of woman. I have a physical need of the earth; and it must not be denied much longer. Everything now points that way. It is not only my own immediate need, but the need to which all my thinking, all my experience, all my desires for the future drive me: everything points the same way now. How to continue a positive step towards the goal with the reckoning on V. as living?

December 21st. The vital thing is belief. If there were 1 chance in 100, 1 in 1,000 of V.'s getting better, or of her ceasing to get worse; or if there were not and I believed there was, then I could somehow fling myself into the struggle. But I can't believe this. How can I? Wingfield tells me that the last bolt is shot. And that to me is final. Max, apparently, can draw on something deeper, feels in himself an active power to drive back the onset of disease. I don't doubt, but I *can't* believe it. I should like to make way for him: but so far it's not possible. V. wants me, not him. The only thing to do is to tell her: that I have, and feel I have, no power, while he has, or feels he has. And I must tell him that I propose to tell her this.

December 22nd. V. agreed that Max should come while I go away for 3–4 days with James.* I ought to go away: the machine is really running down.

January 7th, 1931. V. now depends completely on Max, and I, if anything, am a hindrance. The situation recalls that with Katherine in August–September 1922, but with the *mighty* difference—that whereas I mistrusted Orage and Ouspensky, I trust Max implicitly. That doesn't necessarily make it *easier* to die the death involved in the whole situation; but it may make the death more fruitful. It's all very strange. There is nothing for me except to be passive—to have no resistance. I have none. Tired beyond words . . . Max is coming again on Saturday.

---

* Dr James Carruthers Young.

Meanwhile my mother's stern nurse, Sister Verity, had been replaced by Miss Cockbayne. Then, during the next three months, as my mother grew weaker, the Plowmans took her to their house in London where my father visited her as often as he could. There she died without my father being there.

March 30th, 1931.   Weg is watching at my elbow while I write this, before breakfast. Max rang me up first thing this morning to say that V. died early this morning.

April 1st.   . . . I told the children. Weg thought a little while, and said: 'It's a good thing you didn't die, Dadda. Then we should only have had Maud [a nurse] and Miss Cockbayne.' And Col, as usual going to extremes, said, 'If Maud and Miss Cockbayne had died too . . .' 'I expect,' said Weg, 'that we should have found another house to go in.' I don't think that it meant anything to Col. But Weg did feel something: I saw her —they were both on my knee—going red, and about to cry. But she didn't. But she came to me afterwards in the kitchen and hugged me tight and gave me two big kisses; then she pulled my head down and said: 'If Mamma were here I should do that to her.'

The winds blow from the east and down my memories of a parasol over a lady who walked slowly in a dress of brown and amber and orange and pink over our lawn. I saw her walk away into a sunbeam, so lightly, and disappear for ever. 'Your Mamma is dead.' Those were my father's words when, at the age of six, I sat on his left knee and my brother on his right. I looked out of the window and over the lawn and saw her walking, disappearing. Perhaps she was going over to tea with the next-door neighbours, I wondered? It was a little strange. Did I miss her hard cough, the low, sad voice calling, 'Golly!'? Did I miss the crimson silken sea of the eiderdown on her bed into which I would plunge with delight and heave myself over to look into the little green book of *Alice in Wonderland*? No. She took her place among the photographs, a grave profile. Mamma. Her name was rarely mentioned. There were two photographs that were almost one. Violet? Who spoke of Violet? It was Katherine who came, strong and striding from beyond and occupied quite naturally the throne of honour, saying, '*I* am here.'

On Saturday, 23rd May of that same year, my father wrote in his Journal that he must now '*be* wise actively' and married Miss Cockbayne.

*   *   *

'Old Ada Co'bayne,
Old Ada Co'bayne,
Go, go, go to Spain,
Never come back to us again!'

Col and I chanted dancing round the pump in the yard at South Acre.

'Now stop it, you children, stop it!' cried Betty.

We quietened down immediately. Perhaps we had premonitions.

Then we moved again, this time to the Old Rectory at Larling in Norfolk.

I was to chant and dance no more.

Max Plowman had failed to influence my father in the matter of his marriage to Betty, but he did succeed in firing him with an enthusiasm for William Blake. That autumn, he spent many hours alone in his study, with the photographs of his two dead wives beside his desk, mourning them as he prepared his book on Blake which was to be published in 1933. In the afternoons he would work out of doors, helped at weekends by my uncle who often joined us then, and with Col and me following him around, taking care that he did not forget the special treat we looked forward to every Sunday.

September 5th, 1931. . . . Weg reminded me at bed-time that, if tomorrow was Sunday, I had promised to read David and Goliath . . .

September 7th. I read David and Goliath, but there was a great deal of difficulty over Israelites and Philistines. Still worse, 'Who is the Lord of Hosts, Dadda?' 'Oh, he isn't anybody.'

Very cold all day. Set the anthracite stove going in the dining-room. Woodsawing with Richard in the afternoon, after making a rough 'cradle' by the garage. Weg piled the logs, under the beeches; but kept on knocking off work. She was really more interested in some rather fancy work with a knife, cutting up little pieces of apple to feed us with.

Have been working on Blake all day and most of yesterday —Four Zoas. The fundamental difficulty with this—I am convinced—is that autobiography is continually mingled with myth: I doubt whether the tangle is really extricable at all. But I must make a more diligent comparison of the various accounts of the Fall.

Thought, sadly and tenderly, of V.—always 'the darling, the darling'. What love was in her 'Golly!' And here am I, wandering on, with her ashes a parcel in the brown cupboard. But it's sweet to think about her—there's no bitterness in that sorrow. I have kissed the cold, dead lips of two women whom I loved with all my power of love. Truly, they were all the world to me.

September 10th.   . . . Still toiling at the Zoas. Looking at V.'s photograph after tea, it struck me that there was something strange—if not positively foolish in toiling thus in the traces of a man who sought a solution for the problems of living, when the simple fact of early death remains. Eternity would have to be very blessed for V. to feel she hadn't been cheated. Death is no problem for me, personally. I am quite ready to depart. But for V. it was different . . .

I have asked Richard to try to do a portrait of her, and he has taken my two photographs.

2

Storm Clouds

The Old Rectory, in its Georgian sobriety, stood apart from the village of Larling, up a long, straight drive and some distance from the church which was isolated, too, in the middle of meadows. The house was quite hidden from the road and surrounded by its own paddocks and plantations, with some farm buildings at the back and one or two fields which belonged to Mr Lumley who lived next to the village shop.

During the first months we had a series of maids and governesses who all left, the victims of Betty's ill-humour. Our gardener, Cyril Hewitt, was the only one who managed to resist and stayed with us throughout.

Then a girl of sixteen was engaged. She was diminutive with bandy legs which had been broken when she was a baby to make them straight. Her name was Ruby. Although often we had to fetch her back on her way to her home in floods of tears, her size in no wise diminished her courage and gaiety.

Ruby came from a family of seven children who lived with their parents in a four-roomed cottage adjoining Larling school. Her mother, Mrs Batley, was a cripple. Gentle and uncomplaining, she heaved herself from cooking hob to table with her swollen feet in carpet slippers. Mr Batley, a shrunken little man, was a drunkard and always on the dole. They hated him. The children were unusually small except for the two youngest, Lily and Gordon. They were all products of the poverty and deprivation in rural East Anglia before the last war, when the wattle and daub cottages were often painted with tar and the thatched roofs as they collapsed patched with tin.

On Tuesdays Granny Burlingham helped. She had snow-white

hair and was always dressed in black. She came to do the ironing and, during most of April, the spring-cleaning, when everything was hung with dust covers and Betty raged. Granny was a war-widow and lived alone with her grandson, in a cottage along a path beside the stream that wound its way under a bridge near our gardener's council house. Tough and not a little wicked, she was the only one who could endure Betty with equanimity, and Betty had some respect for her.

When I was seven I would stand on the window-sill of my bedroom, dreaming.

The middle of the sash window was exactly the same height as my chin and I would stare across the oval lawn to the meadow beyond, where the great beech tree waved its green leaves in the sunlight. Life was not easy even then. There were already wounds, there was already fear: the winds of destiny were cold. And yet I told myself that I had to live through this, that there was no escape, that my life was irrevocably bound up with my father's and that it was no use fighting against it . . .

There was a wet patch in the big 'Shakespeare' bed in which I slept.

'You filthy child, you!' Betty's voice, strident and fearsome.

My father bent over me to say goodnight. 'And, darling, do try not to wet the bed.' 'Yes, Dadda,' I answered softly, miserably. How could I explain it just happened when I did not know, how could I explain the hopelessness and the panic, not daring to fall asleep lest *it* would happen as I lay cold and shivering in the big carved Elizabethan bed? Dadda must be helped. If Dadda was well then all must be well. Dadda was Mister Man beside whom I jumped over the ridges of Lumley's ploughed field, trying to keep pace with his long strides, my hand in his: 'Mister Man is an old, old man who's only 41!' In fact he was now 42. The chanting came in an early moment of safety when we were on an afternoon walk, walking away, and it would be a very long time before we would be back: a whole afternoon.

Past the plantations with their edges of dried grasses and black-berry bushes, long strides for almost ever, just me and Mister Man. Happiness riding the wings of freedom over the black gulf that was always beneath, waiting to draw me back to the chilly doom of rejection.

Over the stile: 'Be careful, Dadda, you've hooked your trouser leg!'

'Oh? *Have* I? ' The voice half droll, half apologetic, conniving, sharing.

'Wait, keep quite still, don't move. Fancy someone leaving a rusty old nail just there!'

I unhook the trouser bottom carefully. There's not the slightest tear. All is well.

'*Thank you*, darling. You just saved me!'

'Yes, it was lucky I saw.'

Scant words trembling on the surface of a dark flowing river, like little bits of moss and sticks and grasses, only witnesses and participants of a turmoil and a fear too deep to discover.

On and over the Common dotted with gorse bushes and sandy holes of rabbit warrens, bright white tails shooting out of sight, myriads of rabbit droppings hard and round, to be rolled about with a stick, the grass too short to bend in the breeze.

Some of the rabbit holes were so big you could sit in them; the sun would appear from behind the clouds and for a brief moment you would be all warm in the sand. But then along would come another cloud and never seem to go away, dark inside and hovering.

It was here on the Common that the gypsies would come and settle with their caravan for several weeks. Then it was better to keep at a distance, spying from a safe clump of bushes on the little ragged children with their dirty faces as they played round and under their house on wheels; listening to their nag munching in his nosebag or clipping, tearing leaves from the bushes; watching their fire beneath the black pot send up blue-grey curls of smoke into the still air.

Who cares? who cares? The doves coo amorously in the early morning, enfolded in the sunny summer branches. Not we. Not we! comes the reply.

On rolled that summer, in its rural beauty like many another, slow, nearly static, until autumn came again. Betty was growing big with her first child and had not yet unleashed the full force of her latent temper. There was still peace enough for my father to fret against trivial irritations and even, on occasional evenings, to listen to music:

> *October 11th, 1931.*   Put some Mozart and Beethoven on the gramophone yesterday evening. It brought back Violet, and the gramophone played to her in the cloudy room at Max's house. Those were, without a doubt, the most agonising moments in my life. Yet for some reason when I stare back into them I can't see her face clearly—not as it was then, with the pain and strain of death upon it. Whenever I think of her, I think: What does anything matter? What the *hell* does anything matter?
>
> It seems that now all that concerns me really is simply living from day to day—to shoot things and eat them, to plant things and watch them grow. There remains the world of spirit, which I can enter—the great, calm, impersonal world, where all things are, and nothing cares. Between that world and the world in which I live is a great gulf fixed. In the world in which I live, I have neither ideal nor ambition; it is as though all the vital energy of illusion had been taken away from me. Perhaps I should find content were I to withdraw altogether: but I can't hand Weg and Col over to others, I can't simply say goodbye to Betty and her unborn baby. No, no: life must be lived.
>
> *October 12th.*   A perfectly lovely day. Misty intermittently in the morning, but by mid-day bright sunshine. Before she departed I had to have some 'soul-talk' with X. I'm afraid it makes me impatient and probably unfair as well. But I can't do with beautiful, sensitive souls: those I have known, who were truly both beautiful and sensitive, had plenty of human warmth about them: and X. hasn't. I'm sorry for her; in a sense I even like her—but her gush about the beauty of life shuts me up within my bristles.

*   *   *

Surely life must have been different when the village church was not the all but empty monument we found it.

> Rock of ages cleft for me
> Let me hide myself in thee . . .

I stood by my father as his voice boomed out, sad and serious, stood in my gumboots with my knees pricking from the coconut matting we had to kneel on and sore at the back from the flip-flop of the rubber as we walked over the dewy grass of Church Meadow.

> Let the water and the blood
> From thy riven side which flowed,
> Be of sin the double cure:
> Cleanse me from its guilt and power . . .

The hymn book was very large, with large printed characters. Unlike any of the others. And the church was cold and awesome. My father seemed so big beside me in this long-drawn-out business of a church service.

It seemed normal that his hymn book should be different: nothing we did was ever the same as others. Where could we belong? I walked back silent, hand in hand with him. My rock of ages. Boots chafing, chafing in winter as my sandals did in summer. With the chilblains. And the 'poor finger' . . .

A door had slammed on it one windy day at the Old Coastguard Station at Abbotsbury. And I remember being taken to hospital in a bus, with an enamel basin under my hand and the red pool growing, growing in the basin. Lying on the scrubbed table while a doctor dressed the wound. My father was away at the time, and when he returned he was angry because it ought to have been stitched. So it remained a strange shape and he would massage it in the hope that it would grow straight.

Strange symbol! Betrayal of a fatal weakness, fatal wound, with my father doing all he could to make it right. He had *happened* to be away. It had been unavoidable. And the wind from the grey Atlantic had blown just then, and just then my hand had been where the door latch entered. Why? Why must it be? Question that haunted me in the nooks and secret primrose patches at Larling. Why must *I* be? The earth offered up its sheer beauty. Violets mauve and the rarer white, primroses sweet and tender, from pale yellow to pinky mauve, and, between the roots of the beech trees, little bowls of moss which sometimes held dark pools of water, the leaves quivering above in the chill wind.

Earth, please take me! Earth, where can I go? Not back, not in

there, please God, not in that big house, so cold with its cold
corridors. But there was no answer. Only the shaking leaves and the
sighing boughs. After an endless time, at evening fall, I would creep
back through a side door by the deep bushes of holly and poisonous
'snow-ball' and ivy, through the 'paraffin room' where the stoves
were filled from a big tank with a little tap, past the wash-room, and
past the workshop where my father would work at the bench, doing
book-binding or carpentry on wet afternoons. Then I would hang
about, for still I was not quite in the house. Here everything had a
different smell and escape was still possible. Then, into the dining-
room.

'Here's the lily-white hen who never lays away!' The voice came
in waves, as if incandescent, from my stepmother who was dishing
up the meal in front of the sideboard.

'What have I *done*?' Only a whisper. The trapped animal keeps
perfectly still for seconds while the antennae of its instinct seek
desperately for a way out.

'How dare you ask me that! "What have I *done*?"' The serving
spoon quivered over the dish.

I thought rapidly back over the last days. What sin had I
accomplished in secret? Big Puss had had her kittens in the cupboard in my bedroom. I had kept quiet so that they would not be
drowned, and shared their blind warmth as they groped and
clambered over Big Puss's belly. Big Puss. My eye caught her loping
over the lawn in new leanness, her front paw trailing a bandage
—for the eleventh time she had been caught in a rabbit trap; for the
eleventh time my father had bandaged her paw carefully and
expertly with a splint. The kittens. The cupboard. The dark. My
mind leaped over the territories in fear, full of guilt for I knew not
what. For just having been born? Silence. I watched the shapely
white hand shaking tensely.

'I've already told you I'm not having her here!' So it wasn't my
father, it wasn't the kittens. It wasn't . . . I played for time.

'Who?'

'You know perfectly well *who* I mean . . .'

A kind of sullen bitterness filled my heart, a hatred. Hate for hate.
An eye for an eye. The unfairness.

'If you mean Lil . . .'

Then as quickly the hatred died into a pleading for love, for forgiveness. 'She only came to the meadow. She didn't come in the house, I swear!'

Ruby's sister Lily's spotty face and putrid breath, her pale eyes behind the steel-rimmed spectacles, were mine when together we swung ourselves up, standing on the swing as its iron bars screeched. Up, up, up until we touched the higher boughs of the tree and the swing would quiver to our shrieks.

'Coo, Weg!'

With trembling legs we forced ourselves to a stand-still.

'Lil . . .'

Lil looked at me, waiting. I could not tell her she must not come to play. I could not hurt her like that. How explain?

'She . . .' I paused.

Lil nodded.

'She doesn't want us to play together,' I whispered at last.

'Oh!'

I felt Lil's sadness, yet the implicit acceptance.

'That's all right, Weg. Never mind!'

But there was a knot of sickness deep inside me. Lil was my friend, my only friend, who loved me, who accepted me as I was, who trusted me. *She* had driven her away. Why?

'I'll come down the drive with you.' The drive where, gritting my teeth, I had learnt to ride the bicycle Col and I shared, at top speed, until it threw me over the hedge like a bucking horse. The flints and the ruts and the wild flowers in the grasses at the side.

'Lil . . .'

Silently I looked at the bowed greasy head of dark hair. The silence of knowing between us, where no words can enter.

'Watcher, Dad!' A bicycle had gone along the tarred road past our gate, with a little bandy-legged man sliding his behind this way and that over the saddle. Lil's father coming home from drinking his dole.

'Bye, Lil,' I said.

'Bye, Weg.'

Up the drive again I returned alone, under the wires into the paddock, wandered reluctant before going in.

My brother was not back yet. Betty dished up his supper and I took it into the kitchen to keep warm for him. He was with Lil's brother, Gordon, out fishing. He was free. I wondered sometimes why he was allowed freedom and I not. He was a year younger than I. But he was a boy. It was different. Little boys were allowed to do things that little girls were not. Little girls had frocks that soiled; little boys had grey trousers that did not show the dirt. Little boys could joke with their stepmothers; little girls could not. With freedom dancing in his fine eyes, he would deposit fishing rod, bow and arrow and bicycle pump near the back door and wander through the stone-flagged corridors, whistling.

'Take those dirty shoes off before you come in!' my stepmother would cry.

'OK, mum!' came the reply.

'And none of your cheek! Or I'll cuff you!' But her voice had softened as if by magic.

Our grandparents had wanted him named Colin, so he was called Col for short, although his real name was John after his father. Now he held his hands under the scullery tap, nonchalantly almost.

'Should we make a house tomorrow?' he said to me as I stood watching him press his thumb under the spout to make the water squirt expertly onto a mosquito in the sink.

'P'raps,' I said from a dream of a thousand tomorrows.

'In the back woods?'

His dark hair fell over his brow. On his nose and cheek was a black smudge.

'Or we could play Red Indians and attack Lums,' I suggested.

He turned the tap off meditatively. I fetched his supper from the oven. And we went into the dining-room.

'Look out, she's cross again,' I whispered as I gave him the plate. We sat down . . .

'She's mad! The woman's mad!' Did he say it on that day or on another? My father's wide green eyes surveyed the people sitting at the table. His expression was one of helpless despair, anguish and a kind of unutterable astonishment. Then round again to the silent onlookers—our governess, Col, and a young man, a visitor come to 'see' my father, until they lighted on me.

'Mad . . .' his voice died as his eyes settled into mine. No more need of an explanation; just the sharing. I bent down to pick up the broken soup plate. Betty had gone upstairs. 'I know, Dadda, I know,' came the silent response. Again, later: 'But don't look at me like that. *Please* don't. Can't you see she can't forgive that?' Silent words again.

Please forgive. Forgive him for loving. Me for being. Loving is being. Being is loving. Spoken from the past come the prayers, rising up to the present where the mind sifts through knowledge and experience. But when I was a child . . . No, I did not think as a child. I was only a child for five years. Perhaps not even then. And as for speaking as a child, I scarcely ever spoke at all now.

*   *   *

My father, as ever, was able to shut himself off from all this.

Britain's economic crash, with the ensuing misery of the working classes that he saw all round him, filled him with deep compassion and concern. His old dream of Rananim, with memories, no doubt, of his own childhood struggles to acquire an education, contributed also to his developing social ideals. In 1932 he was to publish *The Necessity of Communism*, although he never joined the Communist Party.

At that time, too, he was collaborating with Ruth Mantz on the first biography of Katherine Mansfield.

> *October 14th, 1931.*   Katherine's birthday: she would have been 43 today. I find it hard to think definitely about her; as though I had lived many lives since then. *The Adelphi*— Lawrence—Violet. And the thought of Violet is so much more a pain than the thought of Katherine. Perhaps it's as well that I can't think much about her. Life must be lived. And there is this. Katherine is complete, immortal—not personally mine. She gave me myself by leaving me. The *shock* of that bereavement was the one crucial happening of my life. Everything afterwards grows out of that. And if I go down to posterity simply as the husband of Katherine Mansfield—well, it won't be far from the truth. But Violet—when I think of her, there is always weeping in my heart.

> *Friday, October 16th.*   . . . Every day and in every way, I become more and more completely the revolutionary Communist—the complete whole-hogger. It's queer how astonishingly swift my evolution has been lately: once the constriction of V.'s illness lifted, things have fairly raced along. It's exciting,

and I like it—but I wish I could live to see Communism come and to see *what will happen afterwards*.

Friday, January 8th, 1932.   My business, as I see it, is to create a truly revolutionary spirit, i.e. a spirit of self-sacrifice. Primarily, my appeal is to the bourgeois intellectual—to make him ready. But I don't see how a direct appeal to the working-class is possible. It's not that I shirk it—on the contrary, I would welcome it—but I think that for some time to come, other people will get in the way: partly because they are *interested*, partly because they genuinely suspect me as a high-brow.

3

Schooling

I sat in Mrs Lumley's kitchen watching her bulbous purple nose with the funny little holes over it and told her that my real mother was dead, she died—I said—when she was only thirty-one. The farmer's wife looked at me, her pale blue eyes all filled with tears.

'You por chil'.'

I explained to her that Betty was not my mother. This was all very interesting to me and to her. Then I went up the field looking under the stones for the bag of pink and white coconut chips that kind Mr Lumley had hidden under a stone for Col and me.

That was the time when Col and I had a governess—or rather a series of governesses. One was called Miss Harper—'Harps'. During our morning lessons we sat in the nursery with our copy-books, copying the incredibly beautiful printed script in the lines underneath. When we heard the bell ring at the village school we were allowed out to play, and we had to come in when the bell rang again. The yew and laurel trees that surrounded the lawns were dark inside, with a warm musty-dusty smell. We used to climb into them and wait. The bell rang out down the road. We waited, our hearts beating with excitement until we saw the grey-haired Harps going down the gravel walk below, searching for us in vain.

But Harps came into the nursery one day, her eyes swollen with crying. Came to bid us goodbye. 'She' had been so terrible, so cruel. So it wasn't us. Wasn't our badness. We said goodbye, we felt a little sorry to see her go. But only a little. She joined the others, the maids and the governesses that had appeared then left, shocked and tearful. Our copy-books were thankfully abandoned and we were free.

Then down the long drive on a rainy day in our new brown macks and sou'westers we went to Larling village school. I was very conscious of a solidarity as I walked beside Col. We did not talk. We were going out into the big world—together. Col, being a year younger, was put in the 'little room', I in the 'big' one. We began with Bible reading, then sums, then reading from the much-leafed blue books, *The Children of the New Forest*. I haven't a notion what it was about. I never listened but dreamed, my eyes fixed on Mrs Hewetson, who was head of the school and taught us in the 'big room'. It was a very serious business and I suspected Col of having a better time with the plump Miss Parrott. She rode every day on her bicycle from Snetterton, two miles away. Mrs Hewetson could not be dreamt of on a bicycle but used to walk the hundred or so yards along the road in a very sedate fashion to her modern bungalow. Her husband kept a chicken farm which he guarded with three big dogs on wire runs in the grass. They were very fierce. One dog, Bruce, was a Great Dane whom he loved.

Col and I used to go and dive in Mr Hewetson's corn reserve. It was like a wonderful warm sea and we got wildly excited diving into the continually moving pits and mountains, plunging like fish, the corn running, flowing after us until, when we kept quite still, it would nearly cease, just one grain after another as if a mouse had set them in motion, then down it would rush once more.

On the other side of the plantation, in its meadows and gardens, stood our house. It seemed created to be a delightful home.

But above were the Fates, the Others, like huge immovable mountains with unlimited powers: the Grown-Ups, the secure, the wondrous race of the Elect. And somewhere, lost, was 'home'. Home that always belonged to the others, little girls and boys who wore the right clothes in the right way, who went to dancing classes in pink silk Grecian tunics and bronzed dancing pumps—one, two, three, four round the room over the polished boards. The silk dress I had, so exquisite to touch, I wore once or twice, then it was over. The dress had no more use and anyway I was out of step; heart heaving desperately to do it all right, I found the left foot where the right one ought to be. Delightful piano pounding out the music. Twenty little girls in a circle, twenty silk dresses in different shades of pink. This time it *must* be right. One, two, three *and* four. The great room and its magic overlooked the Angel Hill at Bury St Edmunds. Why couldn't anyone come anywhere near to knowing how hard a heart could beat? Oh, lucky ones who never knew —how comfortable they were, how beautiful the ringlets of those little pink-clad girls brought up softly with chocolate finger biscuits and china tea in finest porcelain: 'One, two, three *and* four. The other foot, please, Katherine!' Unused to the name, I stumbled and blushed, no ribbons and curls, and after a week or so I was no longer taken to dancing classes and the pink dress was left aside. Occasionally, over the years, I took it out and looked at it, stroking it. Each year it became smaller until, like that very blush of mine, it disappeared into the might-have-been, into the brief happening, brief excursion into a world evanescent as thistledown.

At school, in the 'big room', I copied out poems from R. L. Stevenson's *A Child's Garden of Verses* and passed them off as my own. I always got an 'excellent'. For Mrs Hewetson, no doubt, anything that came from the Old Rectory was incomprehensible, therefore likely to be excellent. I dreamed away the days watching the little round brown mole she had on the side of her cheek. It was very strange. It made her different and rather awe-inspiring. Once Col and I asked her what it was and touched it. She was too taken aback at our *faux-pas* to answer. Primly she would walk down the road in navy-blue, always at the same hour, for year after year, between her school and the impeccable bungalow with doylies and occasional tables set about it, as if on purpose to trip you up. And Mr Hewetson, with his bigness and nice kind face like his dog Bruce's, would sit among the tables looking queer and out of place, but smiling in his blue eyes.

I wished he liked me, but I thought he didn't. He seemed to be judging me and of course I could not come up to the mark. All the right, nice people seemed to judge me and look into my black heart and find it bad. Indeed, I found it bad myself, so dark and secret. Others were like the sons and daughters of light, gods and goddesses with the sun shining through them. Even Col, with whom I shared many games, was possessed of that light, that candour that shone through his large green eyes beneath the dark-fringed lashes that were like my father's. He had the secret of how to touch life as the sun plays upon the leaves of a tree; a sparkle and a joke would come spilling out with a wanton spontaneity at the lunch table or anywhere, and I would sit in rapturous admiration, tongue-tied or just laughing weakly, helplessly, passively.

'Now, Weg and Col.' My father's voice came stern from the head of the table. And the universe collapsed. A great pain in my heart mounted, restricting my throat, preventing me from swallowing. Fiercely I would will the pain away. 'Why? Why? Why?' I muttered, screamed desperately in silence: 'You fool. Stop it!' But the pain grew, a monstrous thing, bringing the flush upwards—my neck, my ears, my cheeks now scarlet—and, worst of all, the tears pricking and burning at the back of my eyes until they were swimming, brimming over and rolling out over my cheeks, plop, plop onto the plate. 'God, God, stop them, *please*.' But the God of little children was heedless. I could not budge. I could not leave the table. My head bent lower and lower.

Then my father's voice again, from far off and yet so near. His tender, worried sigh. 'Oh, *darling*.' This of course made things worse than ever. 'Cure me, cure me, oh God!' I would pray. But there was no cure for the weakness I despised and hated. The appalling truth was that no one had this effect on me except my father. It was as if we were bound by an invisible thread, bound in the inner heart of hearts where reason and logic have no place.

> I had a dove and the sweet dove died,
> And I have thought it died of grieving:
> O, what could it grieve for? Its feet were tied,
> With a silken thread of my own hand's weaving . . .*

Into the dark forest of the unknown I stared, rejected by the blue-eyed gods of light. My soul became part of the dark; I had no place except in that forest. And in that forest I made my home, out of deep silence, a stillness disturbed only by the flutter of a friendly little wren flitting to its mossy nest or the wild hoot of the owl. The great elms flung their branches into the night and, far above, the moon raced drunken and amorous behind the great clouds.

Earth, I turned to the earth. The earth alone could receive me because she received ALL. That was the only certainty. Death. The cold spring breeze bent the young grasses over last year's worn-out and empty beech-nut husks, and under the stones crawled the friendly wood-lice into the moist dark.

'Please, God, help me!' And the silence round about gave no

* John Keats, *Song* ('I had a dove').

reply. But at least it neither rejected nor attacked. In its very negativism there was some comfort. The earth did not criticise. It knew. It was paradoxically the great mystery and the absolutely obvious. It was not God but of God.

So the dark days had begun. I knew not when the heavens had not been threatening. I could not remember. No matter. It was the *now* time that counted. The great rolling clouds built up black over the horizon and sped eternally above.

And, just as eternally, it seemed to me, my father wrote on in the quietness of his study. This 'hero without illusion' truly had none about himself but every possible one about other people, and such idiosyncrasy would never change in him.

Sunday, January 10th, 1932.   Finished a rereading of Eckermann (in Everyman translation). Taking my German copy down and noticing some of Katherine's markings reminded me happily that my first reading of this book was done with her at the Victoria Palace Hotel in Paris in 1922: I lay on the bed beside her and we read it together. The parts of it I most deeply appreciate now are parts which I could not have appreciated then—things which come under Keats' sentence: 'We read fine things, but do not really understand them until we have gone the same steps as the author.' In particular this is true of the noble conversation of March 11, 1832, on Religion, with which Eckermann really ends.

And this is as it must be; for the birth of understanding (of the 'creative' and 'demonic' in me, to use Goethe's language) came directly out of Katherine's death: there was the slow and painful purification which came through V.'s suffering and death, which was the true perfection of my immediate knowledge (irreligion)*—until now I am a free man—in some small but genuine sense a man of destiny, within measure at least of that queer ideal I once put forward to T. S. Eliot, and which he called so 'terribly high'—namely, to be 'a hero without illusion'.

And, I suppose, something is *due* to me, in return for the life I

---

* A fuller discussion of this theme appears in John Middleton Murry's book *William Blake*, 1933 (Cape), p. 272.

have lived. I am a coward, first and last, and yet I have stuck it to the end. I have since 1923 never taken the easy way, always waited for the true way—the way of destiny, my destiny. I feel temptations, at times it seems just as strongly as ever; but it always happens that I don't yield to them. There is something just stubborn in me that cannot write or do what I do not believe. It seems to me that I am a man completely without gifts—a more utterly ordinary person it would be hard for me to conceive, without any conspicuous abilities—and yet, it seems that I understand things which people simply do not understand. It really is a mystery. And it's no use worrying one's head over it—I never do—the only thing is to get on with the job . . .

*   *   *

> Sweet little red feet! why should you die—
> Why should you leave me, sweet bird! why?
> You lived alone in the forest-tree . . .

The intangible thread, silken, that binds more securely than steel chains. The beauty that binds. The innocence of young days.

Do not think that I am comparing myself to the Dove in Keats' poem beyond that of being also a captive, also in essence alone in the forest. I had nothing very dove-like about me. I was wild and would most certainly have been wilful had not my wilfulness been quickly broken. Instead of being clear-eyed and innocent I was deep and deceitful. I became good at lying, a fair hand at thieving. The blue-eyed gods might well look down upon me in reproof. I deserved no more.

But the receiver and the deserver of love are worlds apart. This was the magic of my father's love: it did not require virtue in order to function. It shone as the sun but less fitfully. Other human love had to be earned, even grovelled for: I please you, thought I. You must therefore love me. But my father was the one who knew, with 'knowledge enormous', that to love was more important than to be loved.

At times he would entrance us as he recited, half humming:

On the Coast of Coromandel
   Where the early pumpkins blow,
     In the middle of the woods
   Lived the Yonghy-Bonghy-Bò.
Two old chairs and half a candle—
One old jug without a handle—
     These were all his wordly goods:
     In the middle of the woods,
     These were all the wordly goods,
   Of the Yonghy-Bonghy-Bò,
   Of the Yonghy-Bonghy-Bò . . .*

He made us laugh, too, as he read a passage in the Greek from
Aristophanes, with the croaking of the frogs, 'Racacacac Co-ax
Co-ax'. And laugh and weep at once as he read *The Pickwick Papers*
in his slow, sad voice, with Sam Weller and the terrible descriptions
of the debtors' prison. Beauty seemed to me but a deceiving mirage
and Truth an ugly horror.

For the first year or two our new house was put in order,
redecorated and furnished. And this was the greatest fun. Col and I
went to a big shop in London and 'helped' my father choose the
carpets. Our favourite was a dark red one with big white Qs over it
that you could jump in and out of. 'Buy this one, Dadda, buy this
one!' And my father, to our amazement, bought it.

The Old Rectory seemed limitless with two, three, even four lots
of stairs, and outhouses and box-rooms. And in one of the box-
rooms, under layers of dust, was an old harmonium left behind by
the former inmate, Mr Davidson the parson, later to be christened
by Betty 'Holy Joe'. In the drawing-room, with its big bay windows
and little door beneath them to open right out into the garden, was a
wild bees' nest. The dark, rich honey ran down the wall inside, and
all the time we could hear the faint, fantastic hum of the bees
although we could not see them.

There was a walled garden with peach trees and nectarines and,
over one of the doors, an old fig-tree. The over-ripe fruit would thud
onto the dark soil beneath and lie there for the wasps. The out-

* Edward Lear, *Nonsense Songs*.

houses were potting sheds and stables and a workshop, and a tool-shed smelling of dried earth. Then there was the dairy where stood the great pans of milk from our single cow, and also the electricity shed with the power pump and the rows and rows of beautiful green glass containers which were filled with acid. We weren't allowed near but they looked like lovely aquariums. When the sun shone in the window they glowed with a mysterious being of their own.

Then there were pantries and, passing through them, a quick jab with our finger in the cream was a must. On the cold slate shelves was the wine keg where my father dropped raisins into the elderberry wine, and where the yoghourt jug stood bubbling and working into a mixture he seemed to enjoy as he explained to us that it was *alive* and the alive part always had to be very carefully kept. And the butter churn: holding it between the knees we would churn and churn, waiting for the butter to 'come'.

There was the back kitchen and sessions on a wet afternoon with my father, making 'Everton' toffee. His recipes were always very carefully written out and painstakingly followed. It was so serious and thrilling watching the drops of the mixture as he let them fall off the spoon into the bowl of cold water to test if it was hard enough. and the cracking open of the almonds as we laid them on the baking tin. My father had an immense gift for homely enjoyment and a fund of knowledge about the simplest things. Often it seems to me that he was not really an intellectual at all but a simple man, loving the English countryside, its folk and its ways. It is certain that he had a great need for the true and the real and a great suspicion of all that was clever, artificial, phoney. 'She's too clever,' he would say of someone; of someone else: 'He is stupid through excess of cleverness.'

Round the house were lawns and shrubberies and great bushes of pampas grasses. These pampas grasses I loved, I do not know why. Perhaps because of their name or because of the great bushy plumes, sheeny, generous, or because of their very incongruity, exotic in this Norfolk garden. But they were taken away, like the fig-tree, and the shrubbery behind was more or less cleaned up, leaving only the dark box and yew trees and the ivy running along the ground hiding the periwinkles and spring aconites.

Through the shrubbery ran a little path which led to a gate and beyond it to right and left, were two paddocks surrounded by plantations of beeches. Into these paddocks we often ran, sometimes pursued by Betty, stick in hand, sometimes just out of the sheer desire to run, to feel the wind in your face and jump and gallop over our wide, wide world.

Walking was out of the question. I never walked. To slow down was a kind of anguish, like stilling one's heart. It ran against nature, the spring that moved within me with wild, uncontrollable insistence. The back corridors, with their pink-tiled floors and white-washed walls that led from dining-room to kitchen, from kitchen to dairies, could never be walked along. Absolutely never. I ran to fetch this and that, leaped up the back stairs two at a time and tried to do the same coming down them, with a squeak of my hand on the banister and the last wonderful leap of three stairs to the bottom.

There is a connivance between youth and the elements which later on we lose and can only occasionally re-discover. The sun and the wind, the rain and the snow are shared, understood, accepted as all part of the great mystery of the garden, which is the only true earth, the only true universe.

Outside and beyond was life, life of the grown-ups, different and not really vastly interesting. It had little colour compared with ours, the natural world. It was all greys and browns and shopping at Boot's the Chemists and Sainsbury's. It was roast beef on Sunday and cold joint on Monday and cottage pie on Tuesday. It was cod-liver oil and malt. And how could that bear comparison with the filched eggs from Mr Lumley's barn, fried over the illicit oil stove or camp fire crackling damply in the middle of the woods? Or to the rosy apples, also Mr Lumley's, that hung tantalisingly over the nettle-beds on the other side of the garden wall?

'Weg and Col!'

'Yes, Dadda,' we answered meekly. A tone in his voice advised us that meekness was the best policy.

'Come along. I want to see you both a moment!'

'Yes, Dadda.'

My father was sitting up in bed, reading. He had been ill with stomach trouble.

'Now, you two children, did you knock down all Mr Lumley's apple crop?' We looked at each other blankly.

'Us, Dadda?'

Then I remembered with horror our shooting contest. Who should get the most apples down at one go into the nettles beneath. Such red, such distant things could only be targets. You couldn't *eat* them. They were too far away.

'Now, Mr and Mrs Lumley are poor. And I just can't allow such hooliganism . . .'

Like a painter in front of a virgin canvas, my father, while commanding us to compensate with all our savings, filled in with terrible strokes the picture of Mr and Mrs Lumley, struggling farmers, who had been very kind to us.

Indeed they had. Mr Lumley with his penny bags of sweets that he would hide here and there for us on Easter morning, pretending that he knew nothing about it; Mr Lumley plodding behind his horse over the dark furrows. 'Lums!' we would call. 'Hallo, Lums!' He was a good man but rather silent. He communicated mostly in monosyllables from behind his horse's large posterior which trumpeted and sent out wads of steaming dung as its sole reply.

'Lums! Can we have a ride?'

'Well if that ain't Boy Carl! Up ye get, Boy Carl!'

That was when the horse was released from the plough or the rake and plodded wearily home.

But unfortunately for Mr Lumley, he sometimes in our minds took on the form of the Outside Enemy. Certainly through no fault of his own. It was a subtle change that comes about when a grown-up is no longer friend and ally but an attraction centre of all our belligerent instincts. Then an extraordinary excitement possessed us. We were on the warpath. We planned the attack.

We dug ourselves into a coppice near his field, piled up a good supply of 'conkers' and waited, spying out the land. Then we saw Mrs Lumley coming up along the edge of the field. She was rather tall and straight and walked erect, looking bang in front of her. In profile the red-blue nose alone livened the grey-brown clothes. Mrs? But Mrs was, we knew, a different proposition. She could turn nasty. We dipped down in our trench, trembling with excitement. Dare we? But the battle was engaged. There was no turning back, no cowardice allowed. The greater the challenge the more it demanded a plan, a discipline in the ranks.

The twigs cracked, the grasses rustled and we let her pass by. Better to 'get' her on the return. Meanwhile more spying, running from tree to tree, bush to bush, outhouse to outhouse, even to the haybarn. Low whistles to imitate the birds, messages, signs and arrows in the little paths we raked among the dead autumn leaves, morse codes that Col had brought back from his new school.

Had Mrs Lumley known that she was the centre, the cause, the inspiration of day after day spent in great circles, when the imagination lifted into a great elipse upon golden tracks, swooped, dipped and rose, time upon time, wild and free; had she known, it would not have made any difference to her. For her life was changeless and hard and her small blue eyes blinked out upon it uncomprehending and accepting. We, the meteors, partook of the glory of the earth and the heavens. Again and again and seemingly forever we rode above the mundane world, not like Icarus himself but like Breughel's painting of Icarus, when the unique tragedy of his fall is scarce noticed before the wondrous beauty of the immensity of earth and sky.

4

Mêh is Born

On 27th January, 1932, our sister was born. Her name, Mary, soon became Mêh because her crying resembled the bleating of a young lamb. When the day of triumph arrived and Betty's pains began the house hushed upon the happening. The local doctor arrived—'old cauliflower-ears' we called him, because his ears were so large and crinkly—and delivered Betty of the child.

It was truly a wonder of beauty as it lay in the Moses basket—our little sister. One morning my father moved a silver half-crown across her face and the huge blue eyes with their long dark lashes followed it.

'Look,' he whispered. 'Watch carefully.'

And we looked and watched.

Auntie Dot, Betty's sister, arrived.

'Go fetch a pillow, lass, will you?' she said. And I, on tiptoe round the baby, staring, passionately involved, hurried to fetch it. 'Thank you, lass,' she murmured on my return. Those words remained engraved upon my heart. No woman had ever thanked me so kindly. It never occurred to Betty to thank me and far less to me to demand it. Whereas to Dot's voice and gentle manner something within me stirred, stirred with hunger for a woman's love, and thrilled with a momentary joy.

On Mary's birth my rapport with Betty underwent a change. Until then it had been one of mutual tolerance and acceptance. She was a grown-up, subject, like the weather, to capricious moods, and my brother and I had learnt to steer clear of storms. The garden, the fields, our games, our poor governesses and, afterwards, the village school, were our life. That the governesses and the maids left weeping one after the other seemed rather strange, but typical of the mysterious ways of grown-ups.

But now Betty acquired a new strength. Our little sister was 'her baby' that she held apart, pinned to her breast. The tap-tap of her wedding ring on the sides of the pastry bowl on baking day was subtly indicative of new authority in her. The rows between her and my father were more frequent.

At times we were woken early in the morning by Betty's steady whine in the parental bedroom. It went on and on, hour upon growing hour, until it reached a crescendo with screams and footsteps running along the landing, then sobs and Betty shouting:

'You take your two children and I'll take mine!'

My father's sighs rose:

'Oh shut up, woman! Shut up or I'll kill you!'

But Betty had her weapon now. She was not going to abandon it: her baby.

From now on even the adorable yellow roses that clustered in trusses of such lovely abundance over the bay window of the drawing-room; even the weeping ash in the little lawn in front of the kitchen, which served as a cool green tent for tea in summer; even the summer house with its thatched roof whose straws provided an inexhaustible supply of arrows for our bows, and through whose leaded panes we could peer into the dark wood behind; even the great bunches of dewy daffodils that our gardener would bring in for the house and the arranging of them in the antique Welsh jugs; even the ripe peaches that hung before the old red-brick walls —even all these things could not take away the fear that grew ever greater behind those big grey walls.

It hung upon the air like a perpetual storm, perpetually on-coming, perpetually menacing. It was as if my whole being was geared to this fear which, if it did not break today, would surely do so tomorrow, or in the night. Any unexpected time. I knew by the whispered signs, the embarrassment of the gardener, the flushes of Ruby, that *she* was 'rild'. I learned how to tiptoe up the back stairs without a single one creaking. I knew on which board to creep along the landing to my bedroom, I knew how to turn the round brass knob to my door without making a sound, open and shut it as soundlessly again. I learned how to become a shadow, almost invisible. I learned nearly to subdue the very vitality of spring-time that ran through my veins.

Many years later, in 1955, my father, in a letter to Henry
Williamson who had become a friend of ours, quoted Goethe's
'Forward over graves' as one of his own texts for living.

In this year of Mêh's birth, as well as reviewing for *The Times
Literary Supplement*, he also wrote *An Essay on Goethe* which was
described as the best on the subject in English.* He was deeply
impressed by Goethe's receptivity to personal experience, perhaps
responding unconsciously to qualities that he himself possessed.

It was characteristic of him that he should devote as much interest
to the small domestic routines concerning his children as he did to
the issues of the mind that absorbed him in his work. One of the rites
at the Old Rectory was the weighing and measuring of Col and
myself. In front of the medicine cupboard in the bathroom he would
stand us, in turn, with a book on our heads, and carefully pencil the
height we had attained. With equal care he would put us on the
scales, taking off one weight and adding another. Mêh now became
a part of this routine, to his immense satisfaction.

> *March 23rd, 1932.*   It drizzled in the morning and went dry in
> the afternoon. A pity it did not rain more. We put in posts for
> the new orchard fence. Mary weighed 10¾ lb this morning;
> and looked a perfect darling. I am getting just as fond of her as I
> did of Weg tho' without the anguish.
>
> Took up Blake again. Re-reading *Jerusalem*. I will try to read
> him all through this time and get clear the main lines of my
> book. I don't *feel* it will be very difficult—though God knows
> about the exposition.
>
> A violent argument with Balmer† about Goethe. B. said G.
> was not as great a man as he might have been—he didn't face
> his own loneliness—there was some self-violation, etc., etc.
> Which rather annoyed me. I replied that there was no evidence
> at all for such a view. One can only judge Goethe by the G. who
> is extant; and that G. never ceased to grow. That was the only
> test. You cannot judge a man who grows.
>
> To which B. replied that G.'s growth was only intellectual,
> not spiritual.
>
> To which I replied that G. was precisely one of the men

* Lowes Dickinson.
† R. W. Balmer, a visitor from America who admired my father's work.

concerning whom that distinction could *not* be made: in him the intellectual *was* the spiritual.

Do I consider G. perfect? Of course not. A perfect human being would be a monstrosity—strictly an unimaginable being, to me. Positive, creative, growing, therefore imperfect—this is human 'perfection'. Short lives have an incandescence of beauty—J. C.,* Keats, Katherine—which long ones cannot have. Goethe was as fine as we have any right to expect him to have been; so was his opposite and counterpart, dear old Blake. I couldn't say the same of Rousseau.

True, I feel no warmth of personal affection towards G. Neither do I towards Blake. But I don't feel *cold* towards either of them. I want to champion them. But, of course, I feel *raw* about Keats—and about J.C. in a queer way. I can't *bear* anything that is not exquisite in a judgement upon them: curiously like what I feel about Violet—most agonisingly —and Katherine to a less degree.

The fact is I feel that Goethe's wisdom is *wise*; and that's saying a hell of a lot. I should like myself to have that wisdom and something more—a more simple self-sacrifice. But I recognise that any more would be purchased at the cost of a loss. That recognition means that a man really was *great*. It's just at that point that even Lawrence fails. He could have hated less, and been more, positively. *Alles Grosse bildet sobald wir es gewahr werden.* B. wants to niggle *before* he has made the act of reverential acceptance; and that I can't stand: which is, of course, exaggerated.

Betty has been in an ill mood today; I think chiefly because of the hair in the washing . . .

Wednesday, March 30th. A year ago today Violet died. I've been reading the old, bitter story in my journal. And it *is* bitter. It gives me the feeling that nothing matters—nothing at all: to me personally, I mean. Somehow, as though with Violet all my capacity for personal feeling—for personal love of a person —were burned away, consumed in one long fire of anguish. So that now I can only vaguely remember *how* much, how intoler-

* Jesus Christ.

ably, I loved her, and how much, how intolerably, she loved me.

I suppress the temptation to write out some of the queer anger this memory makes me feel against Max. Why should I be angry with him? I'm not really. I don't feel it. I feel only that I could feel it, if I were to think about it all—I mean Max's part in it all.

Well, well. I am 43. And somehow I have a destiny to fulfil: but not a personal one. What do I mean by that? Something. My destiny is just to be used—to be used up.

The thing I know nearest to personal love now is love of my children. And above all now of tiny little Mary. There are moments when I hold her in my arms, and feel surrendered to, overwhelmed by a sort of sweet rapture: *tacita dulcedo*. Oh, bairns are a blessing!

It is quite evident from my father's journal at the time that he had not the slightest notion of the extent of the terrible effect that Betty was having on his children. He who worked himself to the limit and beyond and stoically endured her outbursts was simply glorying in the joys of continuing fatherhood.

Tuesday, June 16th, 1932, 10:15 p.m.   A lovely day; but I am feeling tired—properly weary, I think. I lay on my back on the drawing-room floor at lunch-time and looked up at the pinks and the sops-in-wine; and was amazed by their perfection. Some tune of one of Richard Tauber's songs was being played on the wireless. Richard* was in the armchair. Mary trying to crawl on the floor. Weg 'making tobacco' on my left hand and Col on my right. And it was all painfully beautiful—with the fleeting beauty of life. These are good moments.

Mêh—her name comes from her 'bleat'—grows steadily more adorable. I didn't think I had it in me to love another little baby as I loved Weg; but I certainly do. I think that if circumstances would allow I should go on cheerfully having more and more babies for ever. After all, I feel that I am a fit and proper person to give little children a real start in life.

But there, on the other hand, I don't seem to be able to *care*

* Sir Richard Rees.

actively any more, whether I make a living or not; and that's no mood for a father in 'bourgeois society'.

*   *   *

Once, a few years ago, I had a little female cat. For some reason I did not love this cat as I have always loved the others. She got on my nerves. She was too fawning, she had none of that proud independence I associate with the feline race. Sometimes I even hated that cat. She became ill and still I hated her. I nursed her forcibly, opening her jaws to make her take her medicine, but I did not love her. I was torn between hatred and remorse and pity. It was a vile, sick feeling and the more I hated her the more she came and rubbed herself against my legs, miaowing. She hardly grew at all but in the spring her belly swung between her paws with new life.

Then she became ill again and disappeared. The gardener next door found her in an outhouse, dead. He called to me over the hedge and gave her to me, and I went and fetched a spade, took the animal on a sack into the wood and dug a hole. The sun filtered through the young green leaves, little beechnuts and acorns were thrusting out tender shoots, the birds were singing pure. I stared at the little cat lying on the sack, my heart filled with regret and pity. 'Why couldn't I love you?' I murmured, touching the soft fur. And as I put it into the hole a long shuddering sigh came from its body, the sigh of the unloved, a terrible reproach for all the dispossessed of this earth. I laid it very gently, and very gently covered it up with the soil that was bursting with life, and heavily made my way back up the path.

How could I, normally a fairly kind sort of person, have felt such an elemental passion of hatred for a creature so innocent?

It was a terrible question.

And in a flash, for the first time, I understood Betty. I was like the little cat, fawning, wanting, insisting on affection that she did not want to give me. I was there, a presence, a permanent accusation, speechlessly demanding a mother's love, the love that so many of us take for granted, are even irritated by or worse, this was my profoundest, unconscious need. With what eagerness I fetched and carried, with what docility I watched and learned to cook and do all those domestic things she was so good at; how ingratiatingly I slaved and skivvied for her, instead of doing my homework.

Thus, I thought, I would earn her love. By doing all I could. Mute so as not to anger the gorgon, careful not to encourage my father's expression of his love for me lest that very gorgon unleash its jealous fury. No glance, no flicker of an eyelash would betray the inner me. Poetry I loved, but since she associated it with my father, his books, his world that drove her into uncontrollable rages, I would read in secret, hiding in the greenhouse behind the boxes of tomato plants and mustard and cress, in the warmth of the little oil-stove.

> Many a green isle
> Needs must be . . .*

But I am now convinced that, like the little cat, the more I tried, the more I desired her love, the more she spurned me. She needed someone to fight her, not to acquiesce.

Above all, she could not understand, let alone accept, my father's continual quest for the idealised community life of which he and Lawrence had dreamt, a dream that still haunted him.

Tuesday, August 23rd, 1932, 7 p.m. Reading, rather skippingly, an enormous, prodigious biography of Maurice de Guérin, I have reached the period of his retreat with Lallennais at La Cherraie. A sort of nostalgia for that communal religious existence comes over me, probably because Betty has been terribly bad-tempered ever since I came home—also because I woke up twice in the night to attend to Weg's cough and therefore feel more than usually tired today.

I don't really see why there should not be the equivalent of the old monastic life in our movement† today. For instance, if one could get Lumley's farm, and four or five congenial people to work it, we could surely hammer out a livelihood of some sort. Turn the bedrooms of this house into cubicles for work and sleep as at Caerleon.‡ (I see Betty's indignation—at the final proof that I was completely mad.) It should be a centre of study, propaganda, and above all a place for the formation of a

---

* Percy Bysshe Shelley, *Lines written amongst the Euganean Hills.*
† This was a Socialist movement which he envisaged at that time.
‡ He had recently lectured at an Independent Labour Party Summer School at Caerleon.

John Middleton Murry in the uniform of Christ's Hospital, *c.* 1903.

As a student at Oxford, *c.* 1912.

Katherine Mansfield, *c.* 1912.

Left to right: D. H. Lawrence, Katherine Mansfield, Frieda Lawrence, John Middleton Murry, in 1914.

Katherine Mansfield and John Middleton Murry, *c.* 1920.

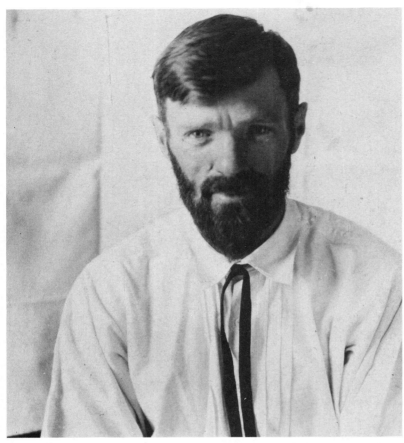

D. H. Lawrence.

Below left: Wingley at the Chalet des Sapins.

Below right: John Middleton Murry, *c.* 1921.

Violet le Maistre as a child, with her mother.

Violet in 1922, from a portrait by K. Jackson.

The Old Coastguard Station at Abbotsbury in Dorset.

Below: The striking resemblance between Katherine Mansfield *(left)* and Violet.

South Acre, Yateley, Hampshire, from a painting by Richard Murry.

The author (Weg) and her brother (Col) at South Acre in 1929.

Violet in 1930.

The Old Rectory at Larling in Norfolk.

John Middleton Murry, *c*. 1933.

revolutionary élite: where equality was always lived. True, most of one's energies would be taken up by sheer hard physical labour: but, for my own part, that would be now by no means a bad thing. I really have no particular desire to write, except very occasionally: and assuredly I should like my life to be infinitely simpler than it is. Why not mugs and platters for meals? Why more than one clean shirt a week, one pair of socks? Why not take turns at cooking simple meals? Why not clean your room and make your bed yourself? I *don't* know.

(Incidentally, I was to notice during one of my father's later experiments that his revolutionary élite lacked his personal fastidiousness in that very simplicity with their 'one pair of socks'!)

Some forty years after this, for the first time, I read in my father's Journals of his vain attempts to cope with Betty. But the following entry failed to reveal even then to my blinded spirit the proof, in his own words, that we both had memories or intimations of far-off days of which we never spoke (one cause, I see now, of Betty's almost animal-like jealousy) and that it was no figment of my imagination:

Monday, August 29th, 1932. Finished the book on Maurice de Guérin. Eugénie's letter to Barbey d'Aurevilly describing his last days is very beautiful. There cracks a noble heart. And there came back to me all the pain of Violet's death, of Katherine's, of Keats', of Lawrence's. When we have done all we can for the world, it will be shot through with the same old pain: the deaths of the young and the lovely and the loved.

Have I said goodbye to this pain? Impossible. Say the word, catch the glance—sometimes in Weg's eyes—and the ache, the impossible longing, comes surging up again: this is indeed *plus moi-même que moi*. And then I feel that I am a ghost, or a body whose spirit dwells elsewhere, with the shades of those I loved.

Hence, I believe, comes that longing to 'retire' of which I spoke to James* and the two Richards† last night. I live as it were, in the world, out of a sense of obligation: the secret 'I' longs to retire, to retire—into death? Yes, even into death. And

---

* James Carruthers Young.
† Richard Murry and Sir Richard Rees.

then it seems cowardly. First, I must see Weg along her road as far as I can: and once that single claim admitted, the rest follows, and I am where I am, doing what I do.

But somewhere, waiting to arise at the moment, is a great weariness: a feeling that I know everything—that the only thing I really desire—what is it? a world of tender, loving men and women—will never be. The loving heart will always be torn to shreds.

Yet I could be content. In a way I am wise—too wise. Nothing means very much; yet everything is very beautiful . . .

Sunday, September 4th. . . . But, of course, one can't settle the problem by laughing, though laughing is a good emollient. Rather paradoxically, the more bloody the rows between Betty and myself (and they have come thick and fast during the last month), the more I am convinced that we *can* hit it off, if only we can find the way. Moreover, I think James and Richard are essentially right in their view that I don't devote enough 'attention' to Betty, *quâ* Betty. That is, I know, a very hard thing for me to do: and a bit harder now that I have acquired a 'Socialist' prejudice against spending money on mere enjoyment as well as a Socialist difficulty in making money. But I must make a real effort to do Betty justice in this respect.

How right Lawrence essentially was about the difficulty of the man–woman relation . . .

5

Fear

'You and your Jesus stuff!'

'Jesus Christ himself . . . wouldn't put up with you as I have done!' Voices rise, crashes and shrieks. Little Mary is screaming: 'Mummy! Dadda!'

My father, white as parchment, his head bleeding, collapses on a chair.

I am cold, frozen with horror. She is killing him.

'Dadda, Dadda! It's all right. It will be all right.' My heart turns to fury, white hot, a fury so deadly as to be beyond shrieks and groans. Still, almost motionless, like a serpent in the grass, my hatred quivers, pure as love itself.

Betty, who has broken a tea-table on his head, comes towards us with fantastic physical strength, shrieking and shaking.

'Get the woman out of here. Get her out!' he may have said then, as on many another occasion. And Hewitt, coming up the back stairs:

'Now, Mrs Murry, don't you take on so. You come along now.'

The passion burning within me was not in the least heroic. It was simply a last defence, like a crab that has been turned on its back. My father was my love, he was mine, my flesh and blood. I was responsible for him. He depended on me. He had only me, I thought. We had somehow subtly changed positions. I, the seed, had become the tree before my time, and my father was struggling for very existence. I was endowed with a strange elemental wisdom, I was his protector; he never had to explain anything to me concerning his own self or his thoughts, I simply 'knew'.

I stood silent, adoring, fiercely loyal.

'*Your* father!' Betty's words were like flowing lava. 'All *I* am is his unpaid housekeeper . . .'

One day, when one of her paroxysms had spent itself, she told my father she wanted to go away. Where to? On a cruise, to Bermuda, she said. This sort of holiday was not my father's style at all and moreover would stretch his purse to its limits. However, he acquiesced; she would go on her own. Shortly before his death he was to describe himself with Betty as 'one third part hero (or saint) and two thirds sheer bloody fool'.*

Having tried Lawrence's ideal of marriage and found that, for him, it simply did not work, the fact that he was only now *thinking* of parting from her is revealing of that self-annihilation which had been at the back of his mind for so long.

His first book on Lawrence, *Son of Woman*, had been published just after my mother's death. It had caused an outcry in the British and American press. Wyndham Lewis devoted columns to 'Mr Murry's sort of sickly and blasphemous clowning' over Lawrence who was, 'except in patches . . . a very bad writer'. E. M. Forster, milder than most, kept the central theme at arms' length while, on the opposite side, T. S. Eliot found the book 'brilliant'. Catherine Carswell wrote *The Savage Pilgrimage* to refute *Son of Woman*, but my father had her book withdrawn for its slanderous and fictitious account of his relations with Lawrence, and was now preparing his *Reminiscences of D. H. Lawrence* as a reply.

It is interesting to note here that prior to publishing *Son of Woman* my father had shown his manuscript to Jessie Wood (née Chambers. She was often called 'Muriel' and is, of course, Miriam in Lawrence's *Sons and Lovers*. Lawrence had broken his unofficial engagement with her in 1910).

On reading the manuscript Jessie wrote my father four very interesting and, in the circumstances, remarkable letters. Since she died in 1944 I feel I can quote the following extract from her letter of 11th November, 1930:

> Having made the reservation that the material you are working on (as regards Miriam) is very distorted truth, I can say wholeheartedly that I think your deductions are most just

* Journal, 1955.

and right. The prime fact of L.'s life, that he was tied body and soul to his mother, is made plain. I thank you most sincerely for your courtesy in showing me the manuscript and I must say that if Lawrence suffered crucifixion he took good care he did not suffer alone.

Although her letters bore out his own understanding of Lawrence, he respected their confidentiality and never used them to defend himself against the baying critics.

Meanwhile Frieda in New Mexico burnt *Son of Woman* before the Phoenix Tree at Kiowa Ranch and posted my father the ashes . . .

Not that such matters had any significance for Betty whose outbursts seemed to have no basis in reality at all:

Tuesday, September 20th, 1932.   Betty is fairly in from the deep-end today: and talking all manner of rot. 'She's a Conservative, and I am not even an English Bolshevik, but a Russian red one. There always have been class distinctions, and there are always going to be. I may bring up Weg and Col as revolutionaries, but she is going to bring up Mary as a Conservative, etc., etc.' In fact, the only sensible thing to do is to hit her; but I don't want to. The exasperating thing is that, I am convinced, she would be far better pleased if I did hit her. And the cause of it all is that Weg and Col went into the drawing-room to play with Beard. It's too silly.

Thursday, September 22nd.   I like her very much: I have a deep affection for her. But at the same time I don't think this kind of life is worth living. Unless there is a radical change, I should say it would be infinitely better if we parted. And I say this with the knowledge that to let Mary go would be the *hell* of a wrench for me.

Thursday, October 6th.   . . . Why is it that in trying to state the truth as between Lawrence and me, I cannot avoid producing the impression that I am trying to prove he was wrong and I was right? Is not the answer that that is what I believe? Yes, but only in part. That I was right and he was wrong is one thing: that he was, intrinsically, a much greater person than myself is another: and I wish to show both those things. Further, in making manifest the real nature of his intrinsic greatness it is necessary to reveal his divided nature. His greatness must depend on the total significance of his works. The beauty of his writing is never a pure beauty: it cannot be simply the object of aesthetic appreciation: it does not allow that attitude to be taken towards it. It insists that we shall attend to, and pass judgement on, the message. And the message cannot be accepted entire. Anyone who takes it seriously *must* come to the conclusion that it is a very subtle mixture of truth and falsehood. The trouble is that people do not take it seriously. It is simply ridiculous to imagine that those who now laud Lawrence—Aldous Huxley, Harold Nicolson, F. R. Leavis —take him seriously. If they did, they could not be what they are . . .

Tuesday, October 11th. Lawrence's *Last Poems* have arrived: beautiful, sad, profound—'The Ship of Death' and 'Shadows'—exasperating. Yet it is no use asking him to be other than he was. What he was is there. Love *and* hatred. He felt them both. He would say that not to feel them both was the Christian lie. And that is so nearly right that once again, one's sails dither in the dropping wind.

And yet: The last grain of truth is missing. When we have (if we have) gone back into the womb, become for ourselves and in ourselves creatures once more, something remains. Beyond our love and our hatred is that which knows us the vehicle of these things. Let them be Gods, there remains that which knows us to have been possessed by these Gods. Beyond love and hatred, there is love. Oh, not of the same kind or order as the love that is hate: not instinctive and impulsive, but serene. As though love-and-hatred were motion or commotion, but Love is stillness, the core of silence.

Is this an illusion? No: it is an experience. God knows what it is an experience of, or by what it is experienced. But it is a fount of healing: 'the furnaces of affliction become Fountains of Living Water.'* It is the Forgiveness of Eternity.

I sit back and ask myself Lawrence's question: How much of

* From William Blake, *Jerusalem*, lines 34–5.

a liar am I? Very much, without a doubt. Very much more than Lawrence ever was. And yet this last grain of truth expands and leavens the universe: the forgiveness of Eternity. I cannot escape it. It has nothing to do with me, and every time I approach it, there is a self-annihilation to be undergone. But there it is . . .

*   *   *

The Old Rectory that was to have been a paradise for a band of little children and visiting friends became an isolated island of hell. A few friends came either from curiosity, bankruptcy, sheer innocence or courage in their admiration for my father. Some stayed for a day, some for a week, but only the hardened intimates for longer. Betty's ill-temper was like a nervous generator that reached such a pitch as to seem pathological. Nowadays such emotional disorders can sometimes be cured, but then, alas, there was no possibility of it.

Like a volcano near eruption her unremitting nagging, hour after hour, night after night, dawn upon dawn, provoked my father beyond restraint. A familiar toneless music, it went up and down, accompanying my nightmares of unspeakable, visionless terror as if my body, pressed to the dark earth beneath the woodland trees, lay helpless under the whining wires of invisible telephones from the unknown.

An animal in terror keeps utterly still, motionless in the long grass as I approach. A little grey rabbit. No movement whatsoever, not a twitch of the ears lying flat against the soft fur and the brown eyes seem misty dull. It looks dead. But how could it be dead sitting there so hunched and rounded? I bend forward and suddenly it leaps up and scuttles into the brown bracken and prickly dead blackberry runners, into its little hole.

Touch it? Not I. My curious hand is enormous, foreign, frightening. I stand helpless. There is no more sound. I am a clumsy well-meaning giant before the immense natural world. Somewhere in the deep, friendly darkness a little heart is pounding but safe.

Feign death, feign indifference long enough and death and indifference settle themselves, squat, unwanted guests. Feign anything long enough and it spreads, a stale poison that engulfs and traps.

Like the rabbit I feigned my way through Larling, through ten years of my childhood. I feigned a stillness in order to survive.

On Fridays it was often hair-cutting day. 'Cut it so the ears show, Hewitt!' said Betty.

Our gardener, who had been barber in the army during the Great War, combed my hair through, gently, carefully. Snip, snip, and my brown hair fell on the face towel; a tiny, gingerly snip over the ears, then:

'Close your eyes, ol' dear.'

And on my forehead the hard, clean, cold feel of steel as he levelled off my fringe.

Hewitt was my pal. He was my loyal friend. He was one of the most delightful men God ever invented. Our gardener from when we first arrived at Larling, he was not Mr Hewitt to Col and me but 'Bodge', and for him we were the 'little Bodgies'. Why the name I do not know. It just was. What's in a name?

Yet there is everything in a nickname. It is formulated with the heart and spirit and becomes worn and polished like old leather. It lives. It is you. It is unique, full of delightful homely memories. So with Bodge. How could there ever be another Bodge? 'Cyril!' said Ruby, cackling over some joke of his when Bodge came in for his morning cup of cocoa. 'Garn, Cyril Hewitt!'

But to us Bodge was not Cyril, or Mr Hewitt, or just Hewitt. He was Bodge, our champion.

'Hi, Bodge! Watchew doing today?'
'Jes' plantin' out them young broccoli!'
'Then what?'
'Gettin' in Primrose!'
Primrose was our cow and he milked her.
'Can I come?'
'Sure—if the missus'll let you!' He winked.
Silence. Why did I always have to be reminded of her? I had not made my bed or helped to clean and dust. Long silence. I stood on one leg seeing how long I could keep that way without falling.
'Well, Bodge, s'pose I'd better be getting back.'
'All right, ol' dear.'
Back to the house, along the cinder paths between the low box borders in the kitchen garden, through the green door, past the rockery and the rose garden, under the ash tree and I slithered through the little doors at the base of the kitchen window.

'Coo, you won't 'alf catch it!' Ruby whispered, pausing as she scrubbed the kitchen table.

'Why?' I brushed my frock down. My heart had missed a beat.

'The missus says you 'aven't done your washin' yesterday!'

My mind went back to the soiled knickers stuffed in the corner in my room. Yesterday? What was yesterday? Saturday? Oh God. Of course.

'What day are we today, Rue?'

'Why, Saturday o'course. Tomorrow's my 'alf day!'

'Then what's she on about?'

But Ruby's only reply was: 'She's real bad today. You look out!'

The dew had still been on the grass when I had gone out and my sandals were wet and my feet getting cold and sloshy inside, as cold as the fear that ran through my being.

I went through the cold stone passage, automatically sliding my hand over the corner table where the back stairs curved and slowly, heavily went upstairs. In my room I sat on the edge of the bed. The carved oaken figures at the head looked down on me with blind eyes; behind the little pillared arches were my sixpence, a few pieces of chocolate, and a propelling pencil in the shape of a little red umbrella. In its curved handle was a glass eye in which, if you held it up to the light, you could see pictures of the seaside at Brighton. Auntie Doll, our great-aunt, my father's aunt, had given it to me. She used to send us big Easter eggs and for birthdays brand new half-crowns wrapped in tissue paper and called my father 'Jack'.

I held the eye up towards my window and saw a sailing ship out on the sea. It sailed, dipped, darted somewhere far away to a great beyond I knew nothing of and could never know. Col and I had little boats. His was blue and called the *Jolly Roger*, mine was red and christened more romantically *Silver Streak*. We painted and re-painted them; they were treasures. But a real sailing ship I had never been in. Perhaps some things are meant to be like that, like the sailing ship in the red umbrella slipping over seas of the imagination, graceful, silent, free, on into mists, carrying the soul on its light, protective wing.

'So there you are, you sly little bitch!'

Betty was standing in the doorway, quivering in her ill-contained anger. 'I heard you! Don't think I didn't hear you last night!'

'Me? What?'

'Oh, you liar! "*Me? What?*" Creeping through the house. "*Me? What?*" Don't take me for an imbecile. I know you. Through and through. Creeping down to your father's study. Think I don't know? You can't fool me as you do him with your whispers and your sly looks. No wonder even your own mother didn't want you! "*Me? What?*" Get up off that bed!'

I sat there motionless.

'Get up this minute!'

I still sat there. Like the rabbit in the grass. Why couldn't I speak to Dadda? Why couldn't I say goodnight to him? The questions, scarce formulated, filled my soul as I saw him in my mind's eye sitting at his desk, his left hand holding his forehead, palm upon the brow, fingers up following the 'flame' of his dark dry hair that still covered a little of his baldness and the scabs that he picked as he picked his way deeper and deeper in thought. The figure slightly hunched and very still, the neat, beautifully formed hand-writing

Katherine Mansfield gave me two separate instructions with regard to her writings. One, in her will, dated August 14, 1922, ran thus:

"All manuscripts, note-books, papers, letters I leave to John M. Murry likewise I should like him to publish as little as possible & to press tear up & burn as much as possible. He will understand that I desire to leave as few traces of my camping ground as possible"

The other, in a letter, dated August 7, 1922, which was left to be opened by me after her death, ran thus:

"All my manuscripts I leave entirely to you to do what you like with. Go through them one day, dear love, and destroy all you do not use. Please destroy all letters you do not wish to keep and all papers. You know my love of tidiness. Have a clean sweep, Bogey, & leave all fair, will you?"

A sample of John Middleton Murry's handwriting.

that covered the thin-lined pages of his writing pads, the warm voice
containing eternal surprise.

'Why, hello, darling!'

'Hello, Dadda . . .'

How could he know the punishments that awaited me for
standing behind his chair? He expected me to come. I felt sure of
that.

How could I tell him I couldn't. How could I let him down?

(Later: 'Dadda, is it true Mamma didn't want me?' The prompt
reply: 'No, darling, of course it isn't true. Whoever told you that?'
Yet it was true. Dadda lied. And I knew he lied and somehow
accepted. No woman could ever *want* me. It was not in the order of
things. My own mother was one of two photographs on the wall.
Photographs do not *want*. She had no flesh and blood. It was not as
important as all that. It was the present that was important. Dadda
was flesh and blood. He needed me.)

'Goodnight, Dadda.'

'Goodnight, sweetheart.'

For a brief moment my cheek would rest against his warm jacket,
then away I would fly, creep, light, soundless, to the darkness of my
room.

One day, Col and I made a map of the Mere. In its midst was an
island. We would swim out to it. We had waited until sundown to
draw our map because then you could see where the patches of
water-weeds grew as the sun caught them dark beneath the still,
shining waters. Then we waited all through the next morning,
swatting horse-flies and pulling Col's canoe down to the water's
edge. He had made it at boarding school. It was a fine canoe and he
had made a trailer for it and fastened it to the back of his bicycle.
Thus we had set off to the Fowl Mere about six miles away from
Larling, very early in the morning, with our picnic bags full, first-aid
kit, and all we considered necessary.

At midday we studied the map again, memorised the weed-
patches, then waded in from the muddy bank. Col plunged in and
was quickly ahead of me. I went slowly; I was not a strong
swimmer. A sort of side-stroke I had half-invented seemed the best.
Sometimes I could see floating on the water's surface a yellow
water-lily. Sometimes I could feel the frightening slither of a slimy

weed about my legs. On, on. I looked behind and saw the bank we had left and the canoe a very long way off and then the island a long way ahead. And I thought of the depth of the dark water and was seized with panic lest I drown or get hopelessly entangled in the weeds. Should I turn back? At least I was certain of the way between all those slimy growths. No, not back. Somehow *never* backwards. This was a battle for victory. Stupid. Idiotic. A quest for adventure, when reality is pushed back to the confines of the ordinary and the spirit is engaged on some proud, mad course. On, on, weak and terrified, my thin arms like frail nothings in the wide waters, keeping above dark, bottomless death. At last I reached the island, exhausted, trembling with fear at the madness of it, and yet elated at the danger. Satisfied. It had been accomplished.

My father, who always took the view that his children must be free, that 'they would be all right', when he learned of this expedition began to have misgivings. And we took greater care he never knew of our penchant for playing on the railway lines. The single line from Thetford to Mildenhall ran between high grassy banks of harebells and through a pine forest. No one was ever there; the grass was sweet and warm and dry and the enjoyment was wonderfully sharpened by the idea of danger: that a train might come, that it was actually in sight, its grey puff of smoke in the distance, the dark knob of its nose pushing towards us as we scrambled up the sandy bank.

Fear was my constant companion. Even in our wild games it was the element that gave them that special tang and flavour that set us apart from our contemporaries, tennis and cricket players. We had not much of a place there. The collectivity that rejected the white penguin had, finally, few attractions when compared with Fowl Mere and the railway line, or the gypsies on Larling Common.

But fear, too, was where the gorgon was. This was different. There was nothing exciting about that. It was a dull, nagging permanency that seemed to grow into the spinal cord, partake of the special fluid and nerve centres, occupy every single part of body and soul, every sleeping and waking hour, the whole of existence. From our games we had always to return to fear that hung, a permanent cloud, over the Old Rectory. No armour could protect us from our own fluttering hearts and strange trembling at the knees. It was an evil fear that few grown-ups could recognise because they could never be completely in its power.

Once, in later years—much later—that same fear and trembling came over me when I was confronted by a poor mad girl moaning and whimpering and shrieking in a fit. Now, as I am only beginning to be able to relive Larling in memory, I realise that this fear was a permanent condition and, grotesque as it may seem to any sane and sensible person, we were enclosed, isolated in that big house amid the plantations of the Norfolk countryside, for years upon end.

6

The Old Tramp

In my being there was a constant war: war against fear; war against weakness. I was caught up in circumstances that seemed quite irrevocable, along with my father. It simply never occurred to me that he might have been able to change them, just as he could make me change from the new school I hated. In my mind he was the first victim and it was my destiny to witness his suffering and to be powerless to save him from it. Upon his happiness all my being became focused. Everything was secondary to that. I asked only to sacrifice all I had for him.

All I had? But I possessed nothing. I dreamed of having £100 to put secretly under his pillow. I was convinced he was terribly poor. When he used to come into the nursery and fish exaggeratedly deep in his pockets for a penny to put into Col's and my money-boxes, my heart bled for him. This was a play-act on his part which he performed to perfection with that wry humour of his. He even went so far one day as to dress up, disguise himself as a tramp, ring at the front door and ask to be taken in for a meal. He did this so well that we were never quite sure whether or not it was a real tramp.

'Dadda, it *was* you, wasn't it?'

He would stare at us in sheer astonishment. He had sat over the anthracite stove in the dining-room warming his hands. Then he twanged an old banjo (our old banjo, *surely*) and talked what we recognised as French. We had stood spellbound. He looked somehow familiar under that old hat. That suit must have been *his* old suit. And it obviously was not Jimmy the tramp to whom he used to give his old clothes.

'It's Dadda!' we whispered.

'Ssh, it can't be!'

Then he thanked us, asked for half-a-crown and we let him out with a mixture of reluctance, relief and awe.

Well it certainly was not Jimmy, because he always stayed several days. We used to spy on him through a keyhole of the potting shed where he would cook his meal on a charcoal stove. He would come once a year, help in the garden and go out on the road again fed and clothed, with money in his pocket. One year he did not turn up; nor the next; nor ever again. So we concluded he must be dead. But the smell of smoke that came through the potting shed keyhole, his shufflings inside and mutterings and ramblings, they can never die.

Not Jimmy, no, the old fellow with a bit of a limp, leaning on a stick, we let out into the dark wintry night. But there was Dadda, sitting quietly at his desk, writing. And that old mack was *his* old mack. It was. It was!

But everybody has an old mack . . . They all look the same. And the mystery remained.

'Dadda, it *was* you!'

His look of amazement.

'Me? When? I don't know *what* you're talking about.'

Definitely: 'It *was* him.'

But the decision we made did not help really, did not quench our thirst to know what he alone could satisfy.

After he had died, I smiled on reading his comments for that day in 1932:

Monday, December 19th. . . . After tea I made myself up with burnt cork and rouge, and twanged the little banjo. I was quite certain—took it for granted—that Weg and Col would see through it in a moment. On the contrary. They were puzzled right inside. Half they knew it was me, and half they were sure it wasn't me. And the knowing not was obviously the more superficial. When I had tumbled to this, I denied vehemently (in French) that I was their Dadda, and kept on talking French. Then I slipped away, washed as quickly as I could, crept down, and asked, 'What's all this I hear about a man?' Acted my part a little while and now they are absolutely convinced that it was not me. And this in spite of the fact that my trousers and slippers were the same, and that Weg was sure of the colour of my eyes, and Col of the bald patch on top of my head! It was an intoxicating experience. Then we had a good time making *all* the noise we could with *all* our instruments. How they enjoyed that!

He used to hum old music-hall tunes during the wine-making or toffee-making afternoons. And he had a way of opening his purse as if it were really his last shilling. The coins used to come slipping out into the little round purse-tray, and he would take out the exact amount, carefully, sliding his finger over the pennies and sixpences and half-crowns.

'Oh,' he would say kindly, 'now . . . how much do you need?'

'Well . . . Dadda . . .'

There would be a silence. How could I tell him what I really needed? It was hard enough having to ask in the first place when he could not afford it.

'Would half-a-crown do you?' he would suggest helpfully.

'Oh yes, Dadda, that's fine. Thank you. Thanks awfully.'

'*That's* all right, darling.'

How could he know the sleepless nights, the anguished waking hours that preceded my asking him? How could he ever guess that his little comic turns affected me so deeply? If only he had dressed up as a king rather than a tramp! If only he had thrown silver in the air with wild abandon! Just once! If only we had gone on a spending spree for that dress of my dreams and shoes to match and white, yes *white* socks!

But we are haunted by the ghosts of our ancestors that stretch down from away back in time, and my father's poverty as a young man, the scraping and saving of his parents to educate him, the sheer hard work, the wresting of himself up from London's East End, marked me as a child, too.

One of my uncle Richard's most beautiful paintings is of his parents. They sit before the blue Chinese vases on the mantelpiece, my grandfather reading the newspaper, my grandmother with a book in her hand. There is a kind of nobility about them, a humble nobility, and it seems to me those beautiful vases are symbols of a beauty and a dignity which was to pass over and beyond them, into my own father's natural beauty and dignity; that the humility which was so much part of him, had its roots in the brooch and lace collar on the simple dress that my grandmother wears in the picture, timid attributes to a femininity never perhaps noticed by any except her two boys. And this vein ran directly through and touched some chord down the years to me. She has her hand on her brow, just as my father used to put his. Above, the blue vases, like a beauty unattainable in their life-time, like the beauty that could have been Larling . . .

But the blue vases were broken, smashed to smithereens, sent screaming through the air, hurtling through the thick, invisible blanket of untrammelled rage that hung upon Larling like a pall. Missiles guided by venom and obscenities:

'You get out where you belong with the ticks and the whores!'

'Shut up, woman!'

Little Mary: 'Mummy! Dadda!'

Screams, the crash of splintered china. The Dresden clock on the drawing-room mantelpiece crumbles, struck to the heart of the loving artisan who made it. The little angels still hold their garlanded mirror, innocent of the ugliness they reflect.

*   *   *

Col stood on the little platform at the top of the workshop steps. He was peeing into a tin that I was holding for him in the cobbled yard below. Full of admiration and envy. How wonderful to be a boy and to be able to pee in the exact spot you wanted. As I held the can beneath the incredible precision of the arc, I could not but share his satisfaction. The workshop itself overlooked Mr Lumley's cowyard, often so deep in squelchy muck that you had to totter and cling round the very edge to avoid falling into one of those amber pools that glittered in straw in the sunlight. In the workshop the smell of wood shavings and the glue-pot. The glue-pot was very nice. Somehow special. It was a double affair, a pot within a pot, with water between the two, and it had a little oil stove all to itself. The sheets of glue were rather beautiful. Amber, too, like the muck in the yard below, shining in the sun. My father would break bits off, drop them into the inside pot and stir them round with a peeled stick over the stove. Sometimes, on an afternoon, we would go up to that sanctuary and watch:

'Watchew doing, Dadda?'

'Ah . . .'

Expectant upon the mystery we stood. We knew he intended to tell us. It was just that he made life so exciting. You never knew what might happen, how things might turn out.

'What's that for?'

'That? . . . ah . . . now mind, don't get yourself burnt . . .'

The pot is hissing out steam into the cobwebby rafters. We follow the smooth rhythmic movement of the plane over the plank and the squeak of the vice at its release, the careful hand strokes, the pale newness of the wood revealed and the shavings building up into a little hill under the bench.

'What's it going to be?' we prompt.

'Ah . . . that . . .'

With infinite precaution he takes the glue-brush and dabs it into the crenellated extremities, pushes them into two other identical pieces so that the shape is like a letter E with the middle missing, then gently deposits it a little way off.

'That,' now there is spunk, pride in his voice, 'that is going to be a cabinet.'

'A what?'

'A *cabinet.*'

'What's a cabinet, Dadda?'

'A cabinet is a chest of drawers.'

'Oh . . . watchew going to put in it?'

'Nails and screws, odds and ends, to keep them tidy.'

'Oh? elastic bands, too, and drawing pins, office things?'

'No, not office things, workshop things.'

My father breaks into one of his favourite songs, an old music-hall ditty:

> Once in a window of a ham and
> 　　beef shop
> Two little sausages sat.
> One was a lady and the other was
> 　　a gentleman,
> Sausages are like that . . .

We listen enthralled. Then:

'Dadda . . .'

'Yes.'

'What's propaganda?'

A white, cumbersome, obstreperous goose he tucked under his arm, perhaps?

'PROPAGANDA! HAH!'

＊　　＊　　＊

During 1933 my father was not only still preoccupied with Lawrence but was also issuing by private subscription a monthly magazine of his literary essays and criticism which he called *The Wanderer*. His book *Reminiscences of D. H. Lawrence* was published in that year, as well as *William Blake*, and he was also contemplating his Autobiography.*

In fact he immersed himself deeper and deeper in his writing as the domestic scene became more unbearable. It was his only escape, and the richness of his creative criticism at that time is reflected in his Journal:

> *Thursday, February 2nd, 1933.*   Montaigne—all day yesterday and today, with immense relish in the reading. By God, he was a human and humane being. I should like to write something really good about him; but I have left myself (I fear) too little time.
>
> Yesterday, John Galsworthy's death. Extraordinary that three of the big senior figures should have disappeared in a week: Moore, Saintsbury, and Galsworthy. He was kind to me, and—far more important—kind to Katherine: but he was never very real to me. I am ashamed to say that I remember chiefly his too immaculately creased white flannel trouser legs when he came in from tennis one day when I went to call at the Grove. And, I'm afraid, he doesn't mean much more than that to me. I doubt whether I have read a single one of his books. How different a memory from Arnold Bennett!
>
> A lovely day—positively a spring day. Jimmy† turned up yesterday. I resumed trenching the little piece by the new Victoria plum.
>
> Montaigne, verily, makes me feel the burden of these days.

* *Between Two Worlds*, 1935 (Cape).
† The tramp.

Yes, there was civil war, and men longed for order and justice—order and justice such as ours would have seemed miraculous to them, no less. If Montaigne could have foreseen a fellow like me, he would have groaned over the perversity of the human race. But the essential security is gone—social, intellectual, moral, religious. I may be a bit more religious than Montaigne ever was, but I am not more humane. Humanity, in those days, had its fixed limitations. There was nothing more to be done than Montaigne did: look after his heritage, treat his servants well, and cultivate his garden. What more could I wish for than the certain knowledge, which M. had, that that was the best? It was verily, 'the good life,' indeed!

And today, to what can I look forward? There is nothing certain that I can hand on to my children—no certainty even of the tiny income of £100 a year each which, when I was 20, I thought so desirable, and therefore desired for them. I wanted them to have all that I had not—to be brought up in a house that would remain a memory to them: to inherit it when I die: to be able to say, 'My Father planted that tree: my Mother's ashes are under this one.' It is all unlikely. The continuity is broken, it seems for good and all. The background is shattered. Montaigne was nearer to his beloved Plutarch and Seneca than I am to him. I live at the fag-end of a world. And yet, with good companions—men who would boldly and bravely belong to the new world and live in it—I should feel differently. Perhaps, in my heart, I *do* feel differently.

As the year progressed, my father may well have felt that, as Gaudier-Brzeska had smashed with bricks the bust he had made of him, Betty's missiles thrown at the flesh and blood John Middleton Murry were all part of the annihilation process.

And with his memories of Frieda and Lawrence's ménage and Dr Young, only a few miles away at Rocklands, experiencing his own domestic unhappiness, he began to think that his life with Betty mirrored a current social phenomenon:

Saturday, July 29th, 1933.   It seems fantastic that at the age of 44, with more than 20 years' experience of married life under what one would call trying circumstances, I am distracted and bedevilled by B.'s behaviour: all the guts taken out of me. A pretty end to all one's experience. And I am deeply enmeshed —by the fact of children. I begin to wonder whether there is such a thing as a happy marriage—or even a contented one. Whether it's not (in the apparent cases) all façade. Lawrence and Frieda, James and Helen, Betty and I—all a mess. Perhaps tuberculosis is as good a solution as any! I feel that I am always on the brink of that ghastly scepticism. But maybe it is that marriage, like all things else, is breaking up. The old social order of which marriage was an integral part is collapsing.

Monday, September 4th. . . . This morning I read Horace Brodzky's memoir of Gaudier-Brzeska—it's not very good; but some of the early pages gave a passable picture of the man. What interested me was a circumstantial account of the break-ing-up of Gaudier's bust of myself (rather 'head') at which, it appears, Brodzky was present. It was demolished by throwing bricks at it. It brought back to mind the occasion of our quarrel—the pathos and tragedy of it.* It seems that there will be quite a lot to put in my Autobiography; but Gaudier and Lawrence will be the only men of genius in it—for they are the only two indisputable men of genius I ever met. I knew them for that, the moment I met them.

There are some documents in existence, by now, which I must consult, e.g. Lunn's *Life of Frank Harris* for a first-class account of the row over James Stephens, when I burst into tears;† Ede's *Savage Messiah* for the Gaudier side of the quarrel between us. Various notes of William Gerhardie's—some scraps of which I have in this journal: the letter of Katherine's which suddenly turned up among my Shakespeare notes of 1921, and which alludes to something I have entirely forgotten. It seems that I might even use that as a sort of Prologue,‡ to show

---

* This whole episode, farcical rather than tragic, arising from the passion my father aroused in certain men, is described in *Between Two Worlds*, p. 221ff and pp. 244–9, and referred to in Katherine Mansfield to John Middleton Murry, 13th May, 1913.

† The story of the quarrel appears in *Between Two Worlds*, Chapter 13.

‡ The Autobiography, *Between Two Worlds*, was in fact published without a Prologue.

how unreliable my memory really is. But the amount of material—once I really begin to get away from my childhood —is appalling. If I am to master it at all, I really must set to. It's exasperating that I have become once more far more interested in Shakespeare than myself . . .

Betty and I had a row. The important thing was, in the course of it Betty acknowledged that both her mother and father had hated her as a small child: that once when she ran to cuddle and clasp her mother she was knocked over. I always 'knew' that the whole trouble went back to her childhood, but now it has been made certain. And I feel this makes a tremendous differ-ence, and that in some sense, half the battle is over, and won. First, because Betty has got to the point of acknowledging this childhood 'conditioning'; and second, because, if only I can remember this, I shan't have half such a struggle to take the initiative in 'forgiveness of ancient (and present) injuries'.

In December he read Lawrence's *Apocalypse* which he found 'on the whole pretty poor'.

Meanwhile, in the face of his domestic predicament, it was small wonder that he had written in the previous month: 'Woman—"the wild will"—really does totally annihilate Man', and even less wonder that, prior to commenting on Lawrence's Letters he was to note:

Monday, December 19th, 1933. Woman—elemental Woman—should be silent: in her love and hatred, silent. Her utterance, in either kind, is shocking. Her moment for speech is when she is calmly alive: not when the demon is awake in her.

Sunday, December 31st. . . . Finished Lawrence's letters this afternoon. By God, they are depressing. His acquiescence in 'the improper public' as more healthy and promising than the 'proper' one is a terrible piece of self-deception. Just to *think* of that 'improper' public—of the people who went to see his pictures when they were exhibited—of his subsequent Euro-pean fame as the author of a book which for its pornography is thrust into your hand all over the continent of Europe. *Gott in Himmel*, but Lorenzo's ghost must be wincing somewhere. Thank God he did write 'The Ship of Death'.

7

Norfolk Days

In 1934 Larling was untouched by happenings in the outside world and the rumblings of the rise of Hitler in Germany.

We had a wireless, but it was only listened to occasionally. It involved having its battery recharged every so often. For this to be done it had to be taken to East Harling, our nearest village with more than one shop, which was three or four miles away.

My father relied mainly on *The Times* for his information.

In this isolation we had, of course, to devise our own entertainments. The only outside one that was regular was the annual village fête which was held in the meadow behind the school. There, at the report of a pistol, we would set off over the rough grass in an egg and spoon, or an obstacle or a sack race. Such a thing as a wedding at the church was a rare event.

Perhaps it was a photograph, perhaps a dream, perhaps only a tale told me by Ruby when I came back from school, that I can see so clearly even now in my mind's eye: the wedding in the Batley family.

The church bells rang out across the meadow. A wedding, with bridesmaids in pink satin with bows of mauve and bouquets of lilies and roses . . .

They trooped in at the church door, the bridegroom looking all stiff and strange; from the sleeves of his tight, dark suit appeared his red, trembling hands. And the bride. Who was she? Perhaps it was Vi, Ruby's sister, dressed in white from top to toe.

'For richer, for poorer.' 'In sickness and in health.' 'To love, cherish and obey.'

Then they came back across the Church Meadow with their crippled mother, large, benign and tearful in her wheelchair and her husband, 'the lil' ol' man', pushing her towards the wedding feast she had been preparing for weeks. Slowly they walked, with Glad and Lil and Rue and Victor and young Gordon. The new husband, shining as a new pin, walked awkwardly next to his wedded wife, Vi, along the cart-track, between the buttercups and cuckoo flowers.

'Cor lummy!' someone shouted at them when they reached the stile, 'if that ain't our 'Arold.'

The groom blushed furiously but threw back:

'Na, you come off it, Fred! You'd a' made the altar afore me but ya doesn't!'

Fred guffawed, but his slow mind could not think up a good answer to that one, so he twirled his bicycle pedal and followed the band down the tarred road, soft in the hot sun, to where the marquee was pitched in the field at the back of the school, in the hope of liberal refreshments . . .

*   *   *

A little taken aback by the broad Norfolk accents my brother and I had acquired at Larling school, my father despatched us to boarding schools. I was nine at the time.

Meanwhile Adolf Hitler had now completed his long march to the Wilhemstrasse to make himself the acclaimed Führer of Germany. The Third Reich came into existence. The new German Empire was born.

My father was reluctantly contemplating a lecture tour in America (whence he would write to Max Plowman during the coming February that Chicago was 'full of nice people but then I suppose so is Hell').

His reflections on these matters were written, as usual, in the face of Betty's uncontrolled ragings:

Friday, July 13th, 1934. Tonight, at this moment, Hitler is making his defence of the recent carnage before the Reichstag. I can just hear his hoarse voice and the murmur of applause on the wireless: it is *sinister*. The damnable *vulgarity* of that hoarse voice—like a showman's outside a tent. Thus it was in the French Revolution, I suppose. But, as bad luck will have it, our battery is failing, and only snatches 'in the wind' come across. But so far as one can hazard a guess, he sounded as

Granny Burlingham with Col and Mary (Mêh), 1932.

Below left: Cyril Hewitt (Bodge), the gardener at the Old Rectory.

Below right: Ruby and Bodge.

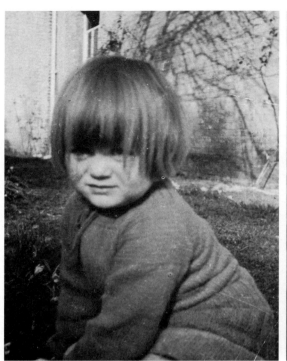

Above left: Mêh aged two, 1934.

Above right: Col with the *Jolly Roger*.

Left: Betty in 1936.

Weg (aged 11), Col (10) and Mêh (4)
in 1936.

Max Plowman, *c.* 1936.

Sir Richard Rees in later life — a freqent visitor and staunch friend.

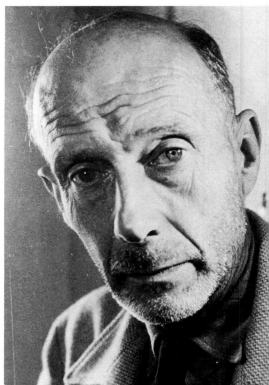

Louise Simon in 1936.

Weg in Liège with Tante Maria, 1936.

Betty returning from a cruise, 1937.

Below left: Weg, Mêh and Col, 1937.

Below right: Betty with David.

Weg, aged 16, while staying with Winifred Trimby at Welwyn Garden City in 1941.

John Middleton Murry, c. 1946.

Mary Gamble c. 1946, later to become the fourth Mrs Middleton Murry.

John Middleton Murry, *c.* 1954. *Photo copyright BBC Hulton Picture Library.*

though he were on the defensive, conscious of weakness; but maybe I should think that of any great 'demagogue', even though he were at the height of his confidence.

Thursday, July 26th. Rather unsettled—windy and close during the day with one or two short showers. Weg came home for her holidays today: Col is due on Tuesday. Weg left her tennis-racquet and her work-basket behind. It seems to me that she really *is* rather feckless: nor should I be surprised if her mother had been much the same. After supper: 'Are you glad I've broken up, Dadda?' 'Yes, why do you ask?' 'Well, you see I thought I might be rather a *worry* to you.' Very odd. I would like to know what is really in her head . . .

Friday, September 14th. The amazing weather continues. Yesterday a letter from Frieda Lawrence asking me to take Lawrence's body with me when I go to America—I rather object to this sentimentalising over L. when he is dead, at any rate by F. for whom, if for anybody, a living dog is better than a dead lion. But I suppose (if this American trip comes off) I must accept the mission. But I don't *want* to go to America; I don't *want* to go anywhere: I want to live and work in peace at home. I've plenty to do . . .

November 16th. B.'s outbursts on Sunday have left me damned unsympathetic towards her . . . And it was not—by any means—all her fault. I couldn't, and didn't adjust to her expectation. I took it for granted that she knew what I was, and that she would understand all sorts of things in my behaviour that she didn't understand: misunderstood fantastically. I was simply bewildered by her jealousy and her temper. The jealousy I had known in women before was concealed and sugared over: before the naked, unreasonable and elemental fury, arising out of what I know to be no cause at all, I was dumbfounded and horrified. I need not go into it. The record of it, I am glad to think, is in this book. It is what I suffered, and what I had to suffer: and at moments I touched an absolute of despair. I was lost in an utterly new world of unknown experience: where I beat her, and was completely unashamed for beating her—where at moments I seemed to come within a hair's breadth of killing her. (Probably, *that* was an illusion: there is a strange kind of ultimate starry control in these things, so that when one feels utterly given over and surrendered to blind rage, one uses only one's hands, so that there is, indeed, a kind of love in the fury, as Lawrence said.) And, at this moment, I am still utterly unashamed for beating Betty . . .'

*   *   *

For my first term at the High School in Norwich I had two new pairs of pyjamas, one pale orange and the other green, and a rug for my bed which I chose myself. There was also a pile of uniform and a black velour hat. But the blouses had lots of buttons hard to do up and the tie was inextricable. Just as at the village school, I was incapable of taking in the lessons. Try as I might the words seemed to go right through me and fly away, quite meaningless. My socks would not stay up; I lost my things and always forgot the very books I needed; I was a hopeless dullard trying desperately to catch up with the others, the gifted, the beautiful, the chosen; I was the outsider, branded, enviously watching the groups of laughing girls; I was different.

'What does your father do?'

'He's an author.'

'An *author*? (giggles) What's that?'

'He writes books.'

'*Books* . . . oh . . .'

It was obviously not the right thing for a father to do. But there it was. Who is to judge what God does? From time to time a girl pushed my bed and shook it, making it tremble.

'How many cars has he got?'

'One.'

'Just one? What sort?'

'A black one with red inside . . . oh, I don't know.'

'Stupid! What *make*?'

'I don't know. Morris, I think.'

'Bet it's an old one.'

'Oh, shut up, Carrots. Leave her alone. I'm going to sleep.' The voice came from another bed. But I needed no champion for my father. I would have killed the whole dormitory single-handed. Dadda mine.

*A portrait of John Middleton Murry, from a drawing by his brother
Richard Murry, made in 1934.*

'Bet your car's an old broken-down one!'

'Ssh! Here's Beechie.'

Steps up the stairs and along the corridor: the Head of the
boarding house was doing the rounds. Miss Beecham with white
curly hair and rosy cheeks, ample and phoney.

'Goodnight, old bean . . . goodnight, old bean . . .'

She bent over the beds, the lace on her brown silk bosom hovering
a moment for the kiss on the forehead. The ritual accomplished,
away she went.

I fell asleep suspended in helpless misery. There was no hope in
Beechie, that I knew, no hope of succour there.

However, as time went by I was admitted to midnight feasts and
the birthday cakes of those fortunates who received 'tuck boxes'
from 'home'. Again the magic word 'home' that they took so
magnificently for granted. Like busy starlings, our voices hushed,
we gobbled up the crumbs on the midnight hour. It was on one of
those occasions that I decided to run away. Where I was to run to
was not at all clear. But surely not to Larling. It must have been an
early summer night for I remember the big black trees along the
road in full leaf.

I went down the stairs, let myself out of the front door and crept
over the scrunchy gravel that separated the house from the road.
Once out on the pavement, quite alone, I walked along until I
reached the main road. Everything was different and silent and
abandoned, quite unearthly. I stood there looking left and right:
there was not a soul in sight; the sky dark yet with a hint of dawn. I
stood motionless while the immense realisation penetrated my
being that I had nowhere to go, that I was totally alone.

And after half an hour's wandering, I went back to the boarding
house, as unnoticed as on leaving. Back to days of music lessons,
scales and the silly ditties that afflict beginners, to lessons, poems
about hyacinths and daffodils, grammar and problems, history and
geography. Yawning years when I could not listen, try as I might, as
the lessons crawled by into a great bottomless pit of the forgotten. I
forgot to do my homework, forgot my exercise books, forgot where
I should be and when. I lost my clothes and was always one of the
last.

My reports came in: 'Very weak', 'Katherine does not try',
'Katherine should concentrate', 'Could do better'. I would stand

behind my father at his desk as he signed them with little comment. Then, after two and a half years of it, I said to him,

'I wish I hadn't to go to that school, Dadda.'

'Why, darling,' he said, 'if you don't like it we'll find you another one.'

As I stood there, speechless with amazement, it seemed as if the heavens had opened wide and through their darkness shone suddenly a great light, so undreamt of that it was a miracle indeed.

'Another? Oh, Dadda, do you think so? Is it possible?'

'Of course, darling. If you are unhappy there . . .'

The absurdity of the whole thing, the absurdity of destiny to which I had submitted, the misery and loss absolute of those years. Why had I never complained before?

It was all part of the grey Old Rectory; of love and misery and of a sense of destiny. I saw my father suffer and sensed, obscurely, that I was a part of it. I had to share, had to help. It just was. There was no choice.

8

A Summer Holiday

I was still at school in Norwich when my father, having returned from his first lecture tour in America, was preparing himself in his Journal for the 'time of real trial'.

I cannot help but smile wryly at his choice of words. What was his marriage with Betty if not that? But he was referring instead to the brotherhood, the monastery, the Rananim, and would describe a few months later the 'real battle of Life and Death, which is what I mean by Socialism . . . a quasi return to monasticism and retreat . . .'*

This was to be his theme when he lectured at the Adelphi Summer School at Caerleon.† And because the venue was in Wales we were taken to Barmouth for our seaside holiday. Before we left he wrote up his Journal:

> *Wednesday, July 10th, 1935.* . . . I must honestly say that I do believe I have some 'illumination' to spread. If it's a delusion, I must stand or fall by it. I must gather up the threads— Shakespeare, Cromwell and Charles, the Autobiography— and weave my pattern of understanding, so far as I can, to the end. I must be on my guard against the temptation to be 'respectable', even more than against the temptation to be *farouche*. I must try to be prepared, in spite of all, for the time of real trial, which *may* come. I don't see it coming: but no

---

* Article in *The Adelphi* magazine, October 1935.
† Although this Summer School was run under the umbrella of the Adelphi movement, the movement itself did not achieve concrete form until the following September, with the purchase of The Oaks at Langham in Essex. This became the Adelphi Centre.

matter. Unless I keep myself keen, alert, alive, conscious, I shan't recognise the trial when it does come.

Monday, July 29th. At that moment Mr and Mrs Wells arrived. As usual, with these nice and conscientious Lawrence fans, they seem to have been surprised to discover 1) that I am not a shifty ogre, 2) that I *know* more about D.H.L. than anybody else, and 3) that I don't nourish any grievances against other people for thinking me an ogre and a Judas.

Friday, August 2nd, 10 p.m. The family, self included, departs at 6 a.m. tomorrow for Barmouth. I have been trying to get all my postponed letters written before going. The weather is magnificent still—cloudless skies and not a drop of rain . . .

*   *   *

The trunk was packed. Col and I rushed about from nursery to bedroom to trunk. I fetched and carried all the indispensables for Mary who was only three-and-a-half. Col and I had repainted our boats, unearthed our buckets and spades from the indescribable, unsortable mess of wools and plasticine, of skittles and jigsaw puzzles, of dolls' legs and cigarette collection cards, of old copybooks and bricks, that was our toy cupboard. Should we take the ludo or snakes and ladders? We plumped for the ludo—it was longer. Where were the water-wings? By a stroke of luck we remembered. They had somehow got into the bottom of the dress-ups box. And our bathing costumes? But they were too small. The buttons had burst on mine. Could we have new ones?

Bliss. Bliss. The sky was pure blue. Not a single cloud.

'It's going to be fine! It's going to be fine!'

'When are we leaving?'

'Tomorrow, of course!'

'Yes, but what time?'

'Six o'clock sharp!'

'Hurrah! Hurrah! We're going to the sea!'

At dawn we were up. Breakfast was downed and cleared away in record time. Bodge was putting the trunk on top of the car, pulling the rope through here, round there, a good knot and a tug, another tug.

'Well, sir, I think she'll be all right!'

We were hopping about on the gravel, our feet all cold and wet with dew. 'Hurry up, Rue, don't forget your bathing costume!' For Ruby was coming with us.

'Goodbye, Bodge!'

'Goodbye, the Bodgies!' said Bodge, smiling.

'Who's going to sit near the window?'

'Bags I!'

'But what if I'm sick?'

'Come on! Come on! We can change over after that!'

So we settled in the back. The horrible smell of the red leather. Col, Ruby and I. Dadda got in front, of course, with Betty. Betty had Mary on her knee.

One try, two tries with the self-starter. The car was evidently cold. 'Wait, sir, here we are!' And Bodge in his braces was bending over the front, fitting in the handle. One! two! three! It sped round. Nothing. Not a sound. In the back there was sudden silence.

Once more: One, two, three, four . . .

A splutter. Then nothing.

The silence in the back of the car grew heavy with dread. Bodge's face appeared from behind the bonnet, red and full of sweat. My father had got out and looked at the thing, nonplussed. Batteries were discussed. But we sat tight, refusing to budge, refusing to give up.

'Let's give her one more go, sir,' said Bodge, the vein on his temple standing out all blue, his thinning hair hanging down in streaks.

'All right, Hewitt, if you can manage it,' said my father, help-lessly. One, two, three, four, five, six . . . Chug, chug, chug . . . chug, chug, chug, chug, chugchug, chug.

'Hurrah, Bodge! Good old Bodge! Hurrah, Bodge! We're off! Hurrah!'

'Goodbye, Bodge! Good old Bodge!'

''Bye the Bodgies!' Bodge, scarlet, soaked in sweat, stood before the front door waving while the car went sedately down the drive as if she had never been a nuisance at all . . .

Soon we had left known country: the fens, Thetford, Ely with its cathedral that we could see from miles away rising out of the flats. Soon I had left the car several times to retch miserably in the hedge. The jogging, the heat, the smell of petrol and leather turned over my stomach and filled me with a single longing: to arrive—anywhere.

But to stop for ever. The smell of vomit hung in the air and we jogged on and on, the countryside reeling past, towns, hedges, towns and more towns. It was all one. While in the front was Betty's monotonous voice accusing, rising and falling, as endless as the journey itself.

It was early afternoon when we sighted our first mountain, a great blue-grey cone rising as if out of nowhere.

'A mountain! I saw it first!' cried Col. He had, of course. I had been gazing sickly at the shiny nickle door knob, wondering how long I could go without asking to stop the car again.

'Stop! Stop!' I muttered, my hand over my mouth.

'Stop!' echoed Col. 'Weg's going to be sick again!'

'She does it on purpose!' said Betty angrily. 'No one else is sick!'

'I don't,' I muttered feebly. Ruby, Col and little Mary stared uncomfortably. The stench was becoming awful. Stains of the morning's Ovaltine down the front of my dress. My father was pacing the roadside unhappily.

'Gosh, Weg, you are niffy!' said Col.

'Oh shut up, Col,' was all I could think of, never having had the gift of repartee.

'I'm sick of you children!' cried Betty as Mary, woken up by the stopping of the car, began to whimper. I stood in the hedge, applying spit and a dock leaf to where the nettles had caught my bare legs.

Back into the car. The mountains grew more numerous. Blue in the distance. So strange. Beyond them was the sea.

Sure enough we came upon it. At last. The great sweeping bay of yellow sand and the mountains coming right down as if into the sea, and the terraced houses going up at the back. Oh, the lovely sand, so smooth, so clean, and the little waves lap-lapping gently, a frill washing the exquisite little pink and yellow shells so clean and shiny.

'Can we go down to the sea just once before supper?'

We raced down the steps of the terraces to the shore where the sand was cold with evening cold under our bare feet, and where the chill water came caressing, shivering between our toes.

'What shall we do tomorrow?' said Col.

We were in a strange land, miles and miles away from anything we had known or remembered. The holiday stretched before us out of sight, like the lovely stillness of the evening sea that lost itself into the far horizon. We were a king and a queen of centuries gone, invested with unlimited powers as we stood there alone on the beach.

'We could fish,' Col went on.

'Collect shells,' I said.

'Explore. Go right over there . . .'

'We could . . .'

'What?'

'Make a boat, perhaps.'

'How?'

'Bits of wood and things.'

In the mind's eye the boat took form. A shell of a boat with an oar and a sail. Just big enough for us two . . .

'It's getting dark.'

'Look! Did you see that? I bet those waves are phosphorescent!' Col said.

I looked but could see nothing. Just the lights beginning to twinkle from the houses above the bay. Reflected.

'I s'pose we'd better be getting back.'

From the wet to the dry sand. Cold as cold now. We plodded up to the boarding house.

'D'you think it'll be fine tomorrow?'

'Dunno.'

It was almost dark when we got in. Behind us the sea murmured like an enchanter. Incantations. The spotted hump-backed shell at home that we had held to our ears had told of such things. Now they were real. It had not lied.

Half-way up the narrow staircase we paused. Not especially taking in the astonishing collection of uglies that seem to be the speciality of boarding house owners, where their energies are most concentrated, when even a peg is not allowed its simple destiny of being just a peg or a picture frame just a picture frame, where even the pictures make one's heart fail before a certain ideal of beauty. These things did not affect us; merely added to the rich strangeness of the holiday. These did not make us pause.

It was Betty's voice, berating my father for daring to bring her to such a place.

The landlady, Mrs Williams, had a long, heavy face with a scowl.

The meals she dumped before us were worse than mediocre. Col and I got rather carried away with the situation and with the peas that were so hard we blew them across the dining-room.

Fortunately for my father he had to repair to his conference for a few days and we were left to run about the beach, with Betty sitting on the sand in a state of near hysteria. We bathed with Ruby and our water-wings. Ruby's face was puckered with responsibility and concern over looking after Mary. Col fished; I collected shells to stick on boxes and stayed at that invisible limit from Betty: not too far to be accused of sulking or not 'helping', not too near to be a victim. It was a fine psychological line that made existence, if not tolerable, at least a practical possibility.

The fifteen days or three weeks ended at last. Goodbye, sea. Goodbye, Barmouth, for ever. Goodbye, sand, smooth and golden. Goodbye, adorable shells only to be found *there*. On the last day it was grey and rained. We packed into the car. The landlady said goodbye with grim relief.

When we turned up the drive again to the silent house, there was at least the paraffin shed and the greenhouse away from accusations and the torn world of grown-ups. And there was still on the mantelpiece the hump-backed shell which held the sound of the sea.

9

Ambitions

During the years 1934 to 1937, my father was more and more involved in Socialism and his plan to build the nucleus of a new society.

'Young aesthetes toying with Communism, cynical disintegration of the Aldous Huxley pattern or a frightened return to the bosom of the Church is merely lemonade compared with Lawrence's efforts,' he wrote. 'Stars arise like Auden only to sink like two penny rockets because the vital change from Imagination to Action can only be accompanied by self-annihilation which they refuse.'*

As for those powers of 'Action' arising out of 'Imagination', he possessed them in plenty. And just as, twelve years previously, Lawrence had discerned this gift in him and wanted him for the founding of a community in New Mexico, so in 1935 Richard Rees, Max Plowman and my uncle (once converted to his community scheme for England) waited expectantly for him to go forward. But he was diffident. His ambition was not personal.

In September 1935, however, he found a big house called The Oaks at Langham in Essex, not too far from Larling. He called it the Adelphi Centre. It was for Socialists of all denominations, with workshops, a conference hall and guest house. It was to be as nearly self-supporting as possible. *The Adelphi* magazine would one day be printed there, too.

If ever a man was élitist it was my father. It mattered not from what 'class' a person issued, he simply had to be the best: the best artisan, the best artist. The high standards he set for himself he naïvely thought he could discern in his followers. Unfortunately he

* Essay in *The Wanderer*, March 1934.

only saw in them what he wanted to see. Until it was too late . . .

On our return from Wales at the end of August, he began to prepare a series of lectures for a second American tour and applied for the Hildred Carlisle Professorship. His mind was not yet completely made up over his Centre:

> *Thursday, August 28th, 1935.*   Long letter from R.R.* bidding me not be precipitate about the Settlement,† and telling me that my most important function is to run *The Adelphi.* To which I replied that I cannot run *The A.* 'positively' unless I make the experiment with the Centre. I must have a message, and the message must come from experience. Either I shall dry up, or I must do something. Indubitably, I feel I have reached a climacteric. Perhaps, without knowing it, I have become a Mr Facing Both Ways—walking with one leg towards a Professorship, and with the other towards a Centre. Have I reached an acme of self-delusion?
>
> I am deeply convinced that a beginning must be made with a new community; but I can't go forward that way alone. It is impossible, by definition. My 'freedom' is now valueless, apart from that advance . . . I do not really want to write any more, for the sake of writing. I have to do the second part of my Autobiography, I should like to prepare a book on Cromwell and his age, I shall probably write a small book on 'Creative Socialism': but that's about all. The real effort lies in the creation of a centre of community. And so far as any voice inside me speaks, it says that I am as well during the period of gestation in the Hildred Carlisle Chair of English Literature as here at home—perhaps better.
>
> *Friday, September 6th.*   . . . I begin to dither, and to ask: Is it really my business? These young men of the middle-class are terribly discouraging—so utterly 'wispy'. I choose the word because it is the one that Lawrence used to apply to me, and therefore to remind myself that it may simply be the appearance which youth presents to middle age. I am middle-aged: not merely *j'ai passé la quarantaine,* as Stendhal glumly re-

---

* Sir Richard Rees.
† A centre for community living.

corded—I am 46! And yet, I don't feel old—don't feel middle-aged. I feel (God forgive me!) in advance of these younger men: not wiser, but in advance—as though I knew the solution for them.

And so, I feel, I must go ahead: but now, I can't go ahead without *people*. I must have people with me not merely in 'spirit' but in body. We must be doing things—concrete things —together.

Sunday, September 7th.   B. was very sweet today. She admitted she was 'an awful bitch to me', and promised 'she would try to help me in what I was doing': though she didn't altogether understand it, she really did believe in it. And, in spite of all, I do have the feeling that when it comes down to brass tacks, she will help me: nay more, I feel (is this my irrepressible optimism?) that in this plan we *meet*. My Socialism becomes a concrete thing which she can accept and believe in and work for.

Church in the evening for the first time since the holiday. Fryer read the lesson. Davidson preached a stupid sermon—on Faith: which almost made one feel he didn't know *anything* about it—which would, no doubt, be very unjust. He indulges in simple examples which are *silly*, e.g. this evening: 'We have faith when we post a letter.' Good. But, 'Sometimes our faith fails us, and we don't post our letter!' Which is nonsense, and everyone of his congregation must have known it. If our 'faith' fails us in this way, we *register* our letter. According to him, we put our letter in our pockets and wait till our faith in the GPO returns, and then we post it!

Monday, September 8th.   HELL.

Sunday, October 6th.   War between Italy and Abyssinia began on October 4th.

Saturday, October 19th.   . . . It is the crisis, really, first told in this journal when I was writing *N. of C.** and which has avoided me—naturally, for I have not avoided it—so long. I must take the plunge, but I do it as ever, reluctantly, simply

* *The Necessity of Communism*, 1932 (Cape).

because I am *driven*, simply because I know that, if I do not take it, I shall always feel that I have missed the bus. And what, after all, does anything matter? What is this kind of agony compared with the things I went through with K. and V., when my heart was just slowly ground into powder? Suppose we all do come to *grief*, what does it matter? We shall be alive. I shall always be capable (I believe) of earning £4 or £5 a week. It's fantastic to be pusillanimous. After all, this little money I have is all *false* to me. I have never known what it is to feel secure. I am the man who should take the plunge: I'm fitted for it —designed for it. And if, as I believe, something will grow from it, well—what a coward I should be to draw back! All the same, it is a 'march', as Tommy Traddles used to say.

I would like to have written more on this Man—Woman business. I think I discern some basic *rightness* in this impersonal destructive activity towards the Man: some essential and necessary test upon him . . .

Friday, October 25th.   B. has gone to bed in a completely unreasonable tantrum. On Wednesday, I went to London to give the first of the Adelphi lectures on 'Community'. It was quite a good lecture and I think went down well. I was staggered to discover that a very nice Frenchman who was deeply moved by it and insisted that it was a 'historical', and 'epoch-making' utterance, was an official of the French Communist Party! There isn't a Communist in England who would not simply jeer at it . . .

The other interesting thing that has happened is that I have got deeply interested in Wordsworth, once more, and from a new angle. It first began to strike me that Coleridge *owed* infinitely more to W. than I had ever clearly realised; that he was far more a feminine reflection of W. than I had understood: and then I realised that, owing to the influence of Keats on my thinking, I had been for many years essentially unjust to W.W. I had accepted, and intensified, the verdict upon him of 'intellectual egotist', and never really understood how justifiable his egotism was—how solitary he was. I have to readjust my whole conception of W.W. and re-experience him as 'a great man'—add him to my heroes. That is, indeed, a pleasant discovery. It's one of the things which (I think) does distinguish me from the worst of my contemporaries, that I have a tremendous desire to *admire*. To have yet another hero is perhaps as exciting a thing as can possibly happen to me . . .

Richard Murry saw the house* on Sunday—a really beautiful day—and was enthusiastic, as I hoped. It was decided that we must try to buy the park-pasture land in front of the house. Apparently, the contract is now on the point of being signed —£2,475 for the two houses and the two fields—a great deal of money: but nevertheless, I think, a real bargain. In Norwich this morning Fenner Brockway suddenly sat beside me in Lyon's, saying: 'Hullo Middleton!' which (I confess) charmed me. As I was conscious of having stuck to my resolution not to criticise the ILP† after resigning, I felt quite unembarrassed and told him what I was up to. I fancy he had a vague feeling that I was 'getting at something'. Today was almost as beautiful as Sunday: the colours, this autumn, have been marvellous—*are* marvellous.

Saturday, November 23rd.   Rather lackadaisically struggling (oxymoron) to get the lectures ready for America. Fortunately, there doesn't seem to be very much to do, really. I don't seem to be very interested in anything just now—or, at any rate, the things in which I am interested are things which I haven't time really to settle: e.g. *why* did Wordsworth go dead? W. becomes more of a mystery to me than he used to be: for 1) I think much more highly of him as a poet than I used to do; indeed I think he was indubitably a great poet in a sense in which Coleridge certainly was not; 2) I see much more clearly than I did that C. was his inferior—but *why* did he ossify? One could say that the cause was the decay of the relation between W. and C. But why was it the cause? It was (I now think) a much greater grief to W. than I had suspected. But a poet gets over—in the sense of absorbing—such a grief. In other words, I find C. very much easier to understand than W. and I feel that I can't be content until I *do* understand W. . . .

* The Oaks, Langham, Essex.
† Independent Labour Party.

Monday, November 25th. . . . How was it that W., who came *so* near, did not succeed in breaking through his Self-hood, but slowly relapsed into 'the intellectual egotist' that Keats saw in him? Was Coleridge's 'defection' far more grievous to him than he had conceived possible? But I don't *feel* that would explain anything. If the wound were far deeper than W. had suspected it would be, the *final* effect would have been to make W. more malleable, more ready for 'self-annihilation'.

Annette? Had W. somehow (? by his intoxicating association with C.) escaped from that too cheaply? Had he plunged into a creed somehow denied (or felt to be denied) by his own unaccepted experience? Was Duty—in the sense of the Ode thereto—a condonation of his own behaviour, which his more 'ecstatic' faith did not supply? My *feeling* is that somewhere along this line the solution should be sought, but that it is *not* simple. 'The old humbug W.' simply *will not do*. This was a big man, who just could not get through (e.g. W. was quite capable of thinking that *he* bore the responsibility for the death of John Wordsworth—in the sense in which this is the thought of a big man. I do not speak factually, for this was in 1805, and the *gran infinito* had been made before then).

10

America

'Goodbye, darling!' My father bent over me as I lay in bed one evening and took me in his arms.

'Goodbye, Dadda . . . Dadda . . . How . . . how far is America? How long will you be gone this time?'

Heart aching in fear.

'Oh, just about three months, darling. Not so long, really. You be good while I'm away and look after Mary. Don't you worry now, my darling.'

I pull him to me in the dark, the sweet smell, the warmth, living presence of his love.

A great agony and terror heaves up into my throat and makes me speechless.

'Goo'bye, Dadda.'

His dark shadow moves up and away and leaves the bedside, leaves the room, I hear his footsteps down the stairs, through the hall, out onto the gravel path. A car door slams, our new car door. I can hear the self-starter being pulled to no effect. My heart leaps with hope. Maybe it will never work. Once more. This time the engine hums and throbs with the cruelty of a hearty well-wisher to a traveller on a death-journey. The headlights upon my bedroom ceiling swing low, then high, then round like great searchlights into the shades of pain, and the car draws away.

'Dadda! Dadda! Why have you left me? Dadda! Dadda! Dadda!'

But no voice, no voice ever while the tears trickle hot, cold onto the pillow, where abandon with fingers of ice writes out one more chilly truth of life.

At the age of ten, just as we are part of the elements, we *are* joy, we *are* suffering and time is timeless.

Those three months, to my father, meant much more than I knew. I could only dimly apprehend, by an instinct that was childish, that his lecture tour in America was more than just lecturing. It allowed him to breathe, to live differently, perhaps . . .

*   *   *

And when he came back he was indeed subtly different. He had on a new great-coat, snug and thick and warm. There was a new life about him underneath that coat, something exciting, faintly, marvellously new. (Later I was to realise that a lady was the cause.) He brought back with him an air-gun for Col, a snow-suit for Mêh and for me a leather suitcase with K M M in golden letters stamped upon it.

Secretly I was a bit disappointed. What could I do with a suitcase?

But my father had had, I suppose, that idea of economy. His present for me would be of use to him, too, on his homeward journey. Now I am struck by the symbol of that gift. The initials came from the past, from his love for Katherine Mansfield who had died. With my suitcase I was to wander between two worlds—not the same two worlds my father had written about in his autobiography two years previously—for the one that was 'dead' was in a sense unknown to me and the one that was 'powerless to be born' I could not yet discover. Instead I was in a no-man's-land of horror where the one person in the world who loved me was withheld from me.

'All women are shits!' screamed Betty. 'Shits! Shits!'

This time, however, there was serious cause for her distress. The only other notion I had that there was something gravely amiss came one summer's afternoon, during a school holiday.

11

Nehale

The lady wore pale lemon and black. Her name was Nehale. Would it have been better if she had worn any other colour? I cannot really tell, but somehow I doubt it. She was at one of those lovely old hotels of England, in Norwich. And she took my hand. I walked quietly but a little sullenly beside her. I did not like her because she was sophisticated and strange and talked in a strange manner. Her American accent was unfamiliar. She was sure of herself with the elegance of the city dweller, of the cosmopolitan. She took me into the hotel with its green plants and goldfish and silent white-coated waiters scudding over the Axminster carpets like white surf on a rolling sea of flowers.

I preferred a bath-bun in Lyon's.

'I don't like cream-buns, Dadda, they make me sick. Or ice-cream. I don't like ice-creams either. They make me sick, too, and my teeth ache. Could I have one of those shiny buns with peel on top, you know, like hot-cross buns without the cross?'

'Why, of course, a bath-bun. Now you go and choose just what you like.'

'And what about you?'

'Well, let me see . . . yes, I'll have a bun, too! I don't care for ice-creams either!'

Tea in Lyon's with my father—the best treat in the world. I watched anxiously as he shook the pennies and sixpences out of his black Breton purse to pay. Would he have enough? Then we went to see *David Copperfield*.

It was harrowing.

The poor little boy plodding along the road in rags in the pouring rain, leaning exhausted on a milestone. Oh, the wicked, terrifying, terrible world. And the rain on the milestone mingled with my tears.

It was just a film. That doesn't count.

Peter Rabbit shedding big tears because he is caught in the net by the buttons of his new little blue jacket.

That's just a story. Don't be so upset.

The debtors' prison in *The Pickwick Papers*.

Don't cry. It is only a book.

Why so vulnerable? Look at your school companions who forge their way through their lives so naturally, with such assurance, such poise, so unquestioning. How strong they are and enviable in their strength!

Sitting in the lounge at the Bell Hotel near Castle Hill in Norwich with the yellow and black lady, surreptitiously eyeing her thin, painted lips:

'When is Dadda coming?'

'Your father will be here any minute now.' Why did she say 'your father' in that way? He was Dadda, not 'your father'.

'Would you like a glass of lemonade while we are waiting for him?'

'Is it fizzy?'

'Yes . . . I'm sure . . .'

'No thank you, then. I don't like fizzy lemonade except pop.'

'Pop?'

'Yes. Ginger pop. That's different. Betty makes it.'

'Ah . . . Would you like a cake, then, or something else?'

'No. No thank you. It would be bought.'

'Bought?'

'Yes. Bought cakes are never half as good as home-made cakes. Molly's cake, for instance . . .'

'Molly's?'

'Yes. Molly's is special. It's all spongy inside with a sugary crust outside and light, light as anything. I always ask for it on my birthday.'

'And who is Molly?'

'Molly? She's Betty's sister. The most beautiful person in the world. She has lovely long black hair, a little bit wavy, that she does up like this . . . a lovely skin so rosy and white and lips . . . For days we were sure she put on lipstick. But she didn't. They are always like that, perfectly red. And she's the nicest, kindest person I ever met, and she laughs, just any time, just like that . . .'

The goldfish darted about in the aquarium and my father was a long time coming.

'I think, perhaps,' said the lady finally, 'we could take a little walk in the Castle gardens. We'll leave a message with the porter.'

It seemed very grand.

We walked outside. Along the little tarred paths that wove in and out of dusty evergreens.

In silence.

Not really hostile on my part but not entirely trustful. Aware of an essential difference somewhere.

I knew—for Betty had commented on it loud and long—that the lady and my father were having an 'affair'. The lurid descriptions by Betty, down to the most dreadful detail, gave me a sense of culpability. I did not want to be walking beside her now. Yet the descriptions I had heard had very little reality indeed. They did not fit the lady. So I was uneasy. I wished she had never happened.

The buses and cars roared round beneath us. Every now and then there was an iron gate you had to swing open and go through.

'You don't believe those dreadful things you have heard about me do you, Weg?' said the lady at length.

I could feel myself blushing.

'No,' I mumbled.

Why was the path so narrow? Why could you only go down or up it and not sideways? Not anywhere else?

The sun appeared behind storm clouds flooded gold. It was very hot. Gnats and tiny flying things filled the heavy air.

Their life but a day. Black specks on my arms.

'It's bad for you. Very bad,' I heard her say half to herself. I did not answer, partly because I could think of nothing to say and partly because I felt she could not know and had no right to think she knew, what was bad or good where I was concerned. I thought of her little daughter Barbara who was four and who spoke German with her German governess, thought of that chubby face and those brown eyes and the big silly-red bow in her dark hair. How could a woman who put a bow like that in her little girl's hair know what was good for me? I thought, too, of her eldest daughter, kind, fair and freckled, and generous—Virginia, 'Ginny'.

I had been to their house. To Ginny's room. She had a little light above the bed (it was made of orange-patterned wax paper) with a red fringe to it. And she could read as late as she liked.

But Ginny was older. There was something different about her, too; as if she did not have any parents, did not need them. She sat up in bed, reading, secure under the glow of her lamp.

So quiet. So self-contained.

'Can I sleep with you, Ginny?'

'Sure you can,' she would answer. 'Come on.' And I would climb up, snug, too, in the glow.

Ginny did not seem quite to belong to this lady. Why not? Or was it the lady who did not belong? She used to call people 'honey'. You cannot belong if you use words that are just not used, can you? 'Bugger them all!' Betty would shout from the top of the stairs at Larling. Yet she belonged. Like the roof to the house, or the kitchen table. There. Terribly there.

The sun changed from fire to silver-white, a formless, insubstantial presence, while the big black clouds banked up, mass upon mass, remote from the noise of the town and its jagged buildings. Then they closed in over the sun and suddenly displayed a light-hearted golden frill.

Down below in the courtyard of the hotel I could see a figure walking with long, slow strides. Dadda! It could only be he! His head was bowed. He was wearing his grey flannel suit, the one he wore for 'lectures' and for 'America'. It was! It was!

'He's down there! Look! Dadda's there!'

'Ah, yes, honey. So he is . . .' said the lady.

My feet had begun their dancing. Hurry! Hurry! Why didn't she hurry, too?

The steep tarred path flipped under the crêpe soles of my sandals.

The lady moved beside me. Yet so strangely elsewhere.

Giddily the gates screeched open, banged shut. Flip! flip! my sandals irrepressibly gay. Down the winding path. Round. Down again.

'Dadda!' My hand slips into his. Hangs on to his arm.

'Ah-ha. There you are!'

Safe. Home.

There is conversation, serious, remote. I cannot hear. I just hang on. It is all right. Everything is all right. My hand drops into his pocket. Warm.

Then we three go down the street together. We could have been four, five, six, a dozen. It would have been no matter. I am beside him.

We were coming back in the car. The two of us now. It was twilight. One of those long summer evenings of almost perpetual twilight. I was sitting in front. I could not see out very well because I was not very tall—just the top half of the trees and the tips of the hedges above the dashboard. My father always drove with a queer *désinvolture*, a kind of *panache* that did not go with the motor car. It should have been a chariot, perhaps. Or better, a buggy behind a good, faithful, reliable horse. He could have settled back, then, to its gentle jolt while the horse's tail swished away the flies, or responded spryly to the eager trot as they approached the stable.

We drove in silence, the town and the chic lady far behind.

After a while: 'Dadda.'

'Yes, darling?'

He was driving rather quickly now but seemed unaware of it.

'When are we going to the sea?'

The summer holiday at the sea was a mixed blessing. The excitement and wonder of being at the sea was coupled with Betty's unavoidable proximity because we rented a bungalow or went to a boarding house. Except for our trip to Wales we always went to the Norfolk coast.

Of course we children never minded how primitive the place was. We had come to the sea and were determined to enjoy it. It did not matter to us that the bungalow at Waxham looked more like a discarded railway coach instead of being the 'luxury bungalow' that Betty wanted, on the front at Gorleston. In fact we preferred it. A thoroughly good time could be had by all, including Ruby who always came with us; we could eat plenty of Nestlé's Sweetened Condensed Milk and there were no carpets and such like to worry about. But Betty had other tastes which my father could not afford and did not much want, anyway. He preferred bare boards to the expensive ugliness of the tourist paraphernalia; the bare sand dunes to a 'classy' sea-front.

So he answered my question vaguely and not with any enthusiasm and we motored on in silence.

I was afraid of going back to Betty after the term at school, but I did not say so. Destiny was fixed. There were things one simply did not mention. Fear was one of them. So I preferred to think of the sea.

Now the road had sunk down into a hollow and my father had changed gear and we were driving up the other side. So I could see the straight ribbon in front of us going to the top of the hill.

There were pines. Little groups of them. And sandy bowls. Some, Col had said, had been made by bombs in the Great War. And tufts of reed and knolls of short grass where rabbits were playing and scuttering away as we went by. And at the top, behind the pines that stood out black, the sky hung, neither entirely blue nor green nor pink, like a larkspur petal and vast as the sea itself.

But what was that right in the middle of the road almost at the top? That heap like a big shaggy dog, golden?

'Dadda, what's that?'

'I don't know. We'd better have a look!'

He stopped the car abruptly and we got out.

'It must be a dog . . .' I ventured.

But as we approached we saw it was no dog but a woman lying in a pool of blood.

It was the long, wavy, abundant fair hair that had given her the shaggy appearance.

In the ditch was her bicycle.

'She must have been knocked over by that lorry that passed us,' said my father.

One or two people were moving in and out of the cottages on the other side of the road.

'We doesn't touch her. Police'll be here any minute,' said someone.

I stared down at the heap in the sandy tweed coat, fascinated. Blood was running out of the corner of her mouth. But not much. So still, that huddle. A human being. The bicycle wheel could still have been turning. Almost. Was she asleep?

My father took my hand.

'We'd better move on,' he said, 'there's nothing we can do.'

'Is she asleep, Dadda?'

'No. I think she is dead. She must have died instantly.'

The sky had turned a deep violet as we got back into the car.
'I shouldn't like you to die, Dadda . . .'
'Ha!' he laughed, a queer snorting laugh. '*I* shan't die!'
How did he know, I wondered? Why was he so sure? But I did not ask. Only too glad to accept. Since he *did* know . . .

*   *   *

The following Easter at Larling Col and Mêh and I were all taken to the photographer in Norwich for our portraits. Perhaps, because of the situation with Betty and Nehale, my father thought it was the last time he would have his three children together. The misery on little Mêh's face at her parents' constant warring is plain to see.

My father's love affair with Nehale drove Betty, who would never hear of a divorce, to acts of vicious destruction and made it impossible for him to shut himself away with his writing any longer.

The Adelphi Centre was now in existence. In the grounds of that Victorian mansion was a cottage called Little Oaks. It was here that my father resolved at last to live, with Max Plowman and his wife Dorothy. He took with him his desk and books and a few personal things that had belonged to Katherine and my mother and, with an aching heart, took leave of Mêh:

Wednesday, May 27th, 1936. The last day at Larling. Mary has been terribly sweet to me all day—so sweet that it is agony. She has served me in every mortal way, with a love that is simple and entire. She promised to keep Col's puzzle for him, so she put it away in 'her secret place' . . .

On Sunday she was asking me about Father Christmas —whether I liked him? She said: 'I think he's jolly nice—better than burglars.' She packed up a necklace of Weg's in a special piece of paper for her, because Weg would 'need it at the Centre' . . .

Thursday, May 28th. LEFT LARLING. After five years the end, the bitter end, of a chapter. The men came to take my furniture in the morning; by lunch-time they had loaded. All the morning my darling Mary helped me. After lunch she went to rest. At 2.30 I went up to say goodbye. She was still awake. She said to me: 'You won't be gone long?' I should have answered 'No', but I had to say: 'Darling, you won't see me again for a long while.' She said, 'The days go quick.' I said, 'Think of me, won't you?' And that was the end.

12

Louise

In 1936, instead of returning to Larling for the summer holidays, I
went to Little Oaks. My father had kept his promise and allowed me
to leave the High School in Norwich that I disliked so much.

At the Adelphi Centre I found relief and freedom from the
tensions at Larling. My father was pale and worn. He looked so
frail. He had, however, entertained the remarkable idea of a *rap-
prochement* between Betty and Nehale. As a result Betty was to do
her best to wreck his Centre and Nehale went back to America.

In the meantime, although I knew he was under severe strain, I
did not seek to question him. That was the grown-ups' world; it was
enough for me to run wild. As long as he was there to say goodnight
to me before I fell asleep, the rest mattered little.

*　　*　　*

Then there came twelve months bathed in sunlight.

One day my father called me to his desk and gave me a pearl
crucifix that had belonged to my mother. He then entrusted me to a
young Belgian lady who was to take me to her home in Liège for six
weeks to teach me French. Louise Simon was writing a thesis on
Katherine Mansfield and had come to the Adelphi Centre to consult
my father. As I carried my new suitcase which contained all my
possessions, she took me by the hand.

I was a mute, sulky eleven-year-old. For whole days I would not,
could not speak.

We took a train from Liège southwards to a village on the
French border where Louise had farmer relations.

Perhaps it was the adventure but more likely Louise herself that
melted my painful silence.

I ran about the carriage, which had no compartments but just bare wooden seats, as we rocked and swayed and clattered round the bends, through tunnels, past woods and small squares of ripe corn on the hillsides.

'*Viens ici, chérie, viens!*'

'But look, look, Louise! On the road over there! A cart and a *dog* pulling it in a proper harness and everything!'

'*Oui, chérie. Un chien. Tu dois parler français. Viens près de moi et mange.*'

Louise was happy, too. She hugged me to her comfortable side and unwrapped our lunch of *petits pains* and smoked ham and plums, and spread the cotton napkin over our knees.

Larling was far away. No bird released from its cage could have been so delirious with joy as I on this August afternoon.

It was so hot that the backs of my knees stuck to the bench. The train curled its way through forest-clad hills, and how could I resist rushing to the window again as if I would take into my arms all those sun-dappled glades where blueberries grew thick-matted beside the glittering streams? The Ardennes.

Little whitewashed farmsteads with their grey slate roofs stood on the edge of the sloping meadows, and I knew that Louise's eyes were following me watchfully as I looked out and laughed, and she laughed, too.

We arrived at last at our destination: Virton. Outside the station we took the waiting car to Dampicourt. At the back of the Citroën I held on to the shining bar of the driver's seat. It was all beautiful and luxurious as we purred along the deserted country road in the afternoon's ending.

In the village, we drew up beside a door at the top of some steps. There were cries of welcome. Arms were held open. I was kissed on both cheeks and then kissed again.

'Tante Berthe,' said Louise with her arm round me, '*Voici la petite.*'

Tante Berthe bent down and embraced me. There was a smell of warm cow's milk and Marseilles soap in her black and white flowered apron and black knitted shawl.

Then Oncle Auguste brushed my face with his long ginger whiskers and everybody talked at once as I pressed against Louise.

Through the door, at the back of the house, just distinguishable in the fading light, was a vegetable garden with potatoes and beans and serried rows of ripening tomatoes.

Everyone then gathered round the table laid for supper with bowls of salads and dishes of cold meats. Oncle Auguste poured out cool, bitter, golden beer, while the animated conversation rose and fell and rose again in this strange language . . .

So began my holiday with Louise Simon at the little village of Dampicourt in Belgium.

Even now I can smell the cow-dung baking onto the road when the whole family walked the mile to the French border and over it to the bistro for *la petite goutte*. Louise and her sister, Irène, who had now joined us, Oncle Auguste, cousin René.

'*Toi, tu es Fascist!*' I would tease René in my awkward, spare vocabulary.

He made a great play of catching me and wringing cries of '*pardon*' from me with:

'*Non! Non! Je suis Socialist!*'

For in the family there was much talk of the *Front Populaire* and the Fascist menace. The Civil War in Spain was only weeks old. General Franco's forces, supported by Hitler and Mussolini, were advancing on Madrid. In France André Malraux was trying to muster aid for the Republicans. A few days before, the Spanish Fascists had arrested and executed the poet Federico Garcia Lorca. And fifty miles away from where we were walking, the Nazi armies were in the Rhineland.

As I listened to Louise and René in their passionate support for the Republican cause and understood Louise's involvement, the French language gradually seeped into my being.

But now, as the days passed more and more quickly, my dread grew of having soon to go back to England and Betty.

Must I go back? I asked Louise. Her eyes smiled at me behind her spectacles. Would I like to go on staying with her? Should she write to my father and ask him to allow her to keep me a while longer?

We hatched our plan and my father, who was experiencing enormous domestic difficulties at the time, must have acquiesced with some readiness. I would stay with Louise and her parents in Liège and attend the *Ecole Primaire pour Jeunes Filles* where her mother was headmistress.

I breathed sighs of relief. Louise had saved me.

One night, before I went to sleep under the giant eiderdown like a great white puff-ball, Louise came as usual to kiss me goodnight. But this time she was dressed to go out.

'Where are you going?' I asked, possessively.

'Ssh!' her finger went to her lips. 'It's a secret.'

'Tell me! Tell me!'

'*Eh bien,*' and she sat down on the edge of the bed. 'There is a secret meeting. We must know what to do, who we can count as one of us if war comes.'

'War . . .' My heart missed a beat as I touched her pretty green velvet jacket with its embroidered flowers. 'And René and everyone at Dampicourt? What will happen to them?'

'René will go to the Front,' she answered quietly, too quietly. 'But you must say nothing, you understand, *chérie*, nothing to anybody about my meetings.'

I promised.

'They are so secret, then?' I put my arms round her neck and pulled her down to put off the moment when she would leave.

'*Absolument.* It's just between you and me . . .'

At school I shared my bench with a little red-haired girl called Marie-Thérèse. In our pinafores we sat up very straight and quiet with our hands behind our backs while our rosy-cheeked form mistress handed out coloured cards, *bons points* for work and conduct. Lessons were no longer difficult or dull; long divisions no longer dreadful.

At weekends I would walk to the shops with Tante Maria and have apricot tart. Louise's father, le Professeur Simon, gave me lessons in French and made me read aloud as he listened attentively, head on one side, hand cupped round his ear.

Sometimes, with two slices of *pain d'épice* for sustenance, he took me for walks along the river Meuse as far as the locks.

'*Ce sont les écluses!*' he boomed and stroked his flowing white beard pensively.

Then I would have to write a composition for him on what I had seen.

The fair came to Liège, its stalls stretching endlessly in the middle of the town, but best of all was the Carnival. Louise had made for me a warm coat for the winter and a matching cossack hat with a muff. Then, protected with a pair of goggles of orange cellophane with rims of brown plush, I ventured with her into the wide tree-lined avenue where people in masks and fancy dress were dancing to the hurdy-gurdy, and the flying confetti, mingled with the dead leaves, was tossed up in eddying spirals in the cold winter wind.

I trembled with excitement, too, when she took me to the theatre and the lights dimmed in the shadowy red surroundings, and the orchestra searched for one note and then another, and then finally the chorus broke into the lilting song:

> *Le petit mouss-e*
> *Le vent te pouss-e . . .*

O, miraculous days!

Sometimes, on dark nights, I would walk home with a girl of about my age, France Truffaut, the daughter of the Socialist Député for Liège. Then—the height of daring—as we walked along we would tear down the yellow and red posters of Léon Degrelle, the leader of the Belgian Fascists and future organiser of the Fifth Column, who would prepare the way for Hitler's occupation of Belgium.

As winter turned to spring I cut my birthday cake that Louise had made and wished silently but with all my might for there to be no war. The ominous noise of Hitler's marching soldiers that came over the wireless could so easily be in the street outside . . .

How could I not feel, as I chalked out squares for hopscotch on the garden path and watched the purple grapes ripening on the wall and the queer palm tree that flowered for the first time in seven years, that danger was building up like thunder? How could I not fear for Louise?

In Spain, as Guernica was razed by Göring's Junkers, its people machine-gunned by his Heinkels and Bilbao fell, the English language faded from my tongue and mind and in the lowered voices of Louise and her colleagues I knew their plans were being laid for the Resistance movement.

In the end I stayed in Belgium until the school year was completed, and then leaving the Simon family made me sad indeed.

Yet nothing for me would ever be quite the same again. The love between Louise and myself I hid in my heart, a private certainty of the existence of heaven.

In moments of extreme despair—for it seemed, alas, that no power on earth could desensitise me or harden me sufficiently to withstand Betty's onslaughts—I would implore God, who seemed so deaf, for Louise to come and take me away again.

But I can see now that in her patience and wisdom she had saved me: in future, however weak and cowardly I might be, there had formed a tiny unity within me, carefully fostered by her, which even Betty would not have the power to destroy.

    *   *   *

Meanwhile my father's departure from Larling had not been as final as he had thought. Betty used Mêh unashamedly to blackmail him into returning to her. Then she went on another cruise—to Yugoslavia this time—and Mêh stayed (with Ruby to look after her) in London with Mabel Fiertz whom my father had, I believe, met through George Orwell at the Adelphi Centre.

Christian pacifism, my father now felt, was the only way of coping with the microcosm of the warring world (Betty) and its macrocosm (Fascism). In 1937 he met Canon Dick Sheppard who gave him Bernanos' *Diary of a Country Priest*. They planned to tour the country together to rally people to their views. But in October Sheppard died suddenly.

I was still in Belgium when, little by little, as always using poor Mêh as the bait, Betty lured my father back to Larling.

Now he was to go over to the Centre at weekends only. His friends there, bereft of their leader, felt betrayed. Some, as Socialists, did not accept his renewed faith in Christianity. They all wanted him there permanently. However, since there was nothing they could do about it, everyone agreed to use the house for Basque refugees and printing *The Adelphi*, while my father planned a short Summer School at Larling.

Saturday, May 22nd, 1937.   The simple truth as I told Betty this morning, is that she must trust me, knowing what I am; she must either know in her heart that I love her and cannot be disloyal to her, or she will go on tearing herself and me to pieces. Finally and quite simply, love is complete trust, which is Life, or it is distrust, which is jealousy and death. And it's not the faintest use her saying to herself that she trusts me, but she does not trust the women or the men around me, who may 'pull wool over my eyes'. That is just the same as not trusting me. Love is faith in Love. I am beginning to wonder whether any woman has ever felt it. The woman wants to protect, and wants to possess: it's the same motion. Instead of loyally following her man forward into the danger and exposure of innocency, she seeks to drag him back into the protection which is possession. Knowing her own infinite guile, she cannot trust that her man will be proof against it. As often as not she captured him by guile; how then should he not fall a victim to it again? So she becomes a victim of her own Femaleness.

'Forbid all Joy, and from her childhood shall the little female spread nets in every secret path.'*

Monday, May 24th. On the way back on Sunday evening Mary told me she had found two pencils in the drawer by the telephone. 'I thought I'd better take them, or they'd be took,' she said. She is an extraordinary darling—quite unspoiled and serious. Betty said, with tears, this morning: 'I feel you look on Mary as something utterly apart from me, that I had nothing to do with: she's all *you*.' This is not so. I look on Mary as an unspoiled Betty—what Betty was meant to be. She said casually in the car last night that she had never had a birthday cake in her life! That explains a terrible lot.

June 18th, 10 p.m. ... I have pretty well touched bottom now. I earn, and can earn, practically nothing: and I shall obviously have to give up *The Adelphi*. I think there's no real doubt about that. But I don't feel really depressed. I feel that Betty and I have really struggled through to something worth having: I adore my little daughter: my children are all lovely to me. In that simple, bedrock, human way I haven't failed. I'm tired, yes: but I don't worry very much. I should like to free myself of some of my bonds. I would like to get something *real*

* William Blake, *Europe: a Prophecy*, Plate 5.

started with my brother. I think I've spent myself excessively in the last two years: and I'm not quite sure *what* I have learned. But it's not too bad. I wouldn't change places . . .

Wednesday, June 21st.   Back after driving 300 miles to Rendcomb* and back, to see Col. I *was* glad I went. He would have been so terribly disappointed if I had let him down. And, come what may, I'll try to go again next term. More and more I come to feel that children are more important than anything: and that the kind of understanding I have with them is the most precious thing in my life. Children really are *wounded*. And the profundity of Christ's simple doctrine, 'See that ye offend not one of these little ones', is unsoundable. More and more I come to regard his teaching concerning children—his putting of that teaching at the very centre of his doctrine—as the evidence that 'Truly this man was the son of God'.

For children (whatever people may say) love without making any demand—any demand to possess. My children can't be exceptional: yet I am quite sure there is no jealousy among them. None of them want to monopolise my love. But they do feel it—as Col undoubtedly did—when they are not getting their fair share. To put it better, they do ask that their love, which is quite simple, shall be returned: that there shall be the 'flow'. But they ask nothing more.

* Rendcomb College, Gloucestershire.

13

Return to Larling

In August, when I returned to England with Louise, it was back to Larling once more. However, my sinking spirits were somewhat restored by the sight of tents pitched in the swing-tree meadow, the bedrooms in the house transformed into dormitories, long tables in my father's study which was being used as a refectory, and the drawing-room full of chairs lined up for conferences. There was a general air of bustle and pre-occupation about the place and Daphne Deiner, a little girl of my own age, of whom I was to grow very fond, was there, too, brought by her mother who was busy on this project of my father's: the Adelphi Summer School.

We children, Col, Daphne, Mêh and I, all had to share a bedroom and our excitement was boundless. Equally enjoyable were the hours I spent with Daphne satisfying our literary ambitions by composing *romans fleuves*.

Bodge's wife Gertrude, Ruby and Granny Burlingham, all had their hands full, as indeed did Louise and my uncle Richard. My father's then secretary, Miss Watt, and Daphne's mother were equally active: Betty had not yet driven them both away.

When it was over and Louise had gone back to Belgium, my father shut himself up in his study as of old, preparing a new book of literary essays.* His interests were as wide as ever and Katherine was never far from his thoughts. Although Betty did not—indeed, could not—change, and the strain of the life he led was beginning to tell on his health, he himself was full of renewed optimism:

Friday, August 28th, 1937. The Summer School appears more and more as a triumph for Betty, for which I am heartily

* *Heaven—and Earth*, 1938 (Cape) studies of twelve great men.

glad. She really deserves it; and her natural gaiety and skill in management was the real bond that made the school so healthy and rich. Here for the first time we were a living and creative combination; and there was no room for the exotic devotion of unsatisfied women to develop. I feel that there is now the beginning of a *solid* growth: in which Betty has played the part which it was her destiny to play. It's *good*. And, in the simple practical sense, we have sent out a little band of people who are genuinely devoted to *The Adelphi*, and will really work for it.

Thursday, September 2nd. Reading a capricious but informative book on Chekhov by Princess Nina Andronikova Tourmanova, and came with great gratification on this entry from Suvorin's diary immediately after the complete failure of *The Seagull* in Petersburg in 1896.

> Mevezhkovsky, whom I met in the theatre, said the play was not intelligent, for the first quality of intelligence is clarity. I let him understand that he never had that clarity himself.

It fits perfectly with my own brief encounter with Merezhkovsky in Paris (?1922) when he struck me as full of envy and malice—a *mean* soul. It was the night when Bunin was also present and Katherine hoped that she might hear something vivid and revealing from men who had actually known Chekhov: and all she got was Bunin's: '*Ah, oui, il était charmant*'—or words to that effect. There was obviously a great jealousy of Chekhov: far more pronounced in Merezhkovsky than Bunin. In M.'s case I suppose an example of the grudge of talent against genius. I was inclined to be charitable and to suppose that M. had degenerated under the strain of the revolutionary upheaval, so damned unpleasant was the impression he made upon me—as of something rather obscene, reptilian. But now I perceive that he always was a bit of a rat, whom a man like Suvorin would despise.

Suvorin, too, let Chekhov down—in a totally different way—over Dreyfus. In spite of the fact that Chekhov had convinced him of Dreyfus' innocence, *Novoye Vremya* went on violently attacking Dreyfus. Suvorin, who was a man of business, couldn't afford to quarrel with the Russian Government which supported his newspaper. But that's a different kettle of fish, altogether. I imagine that, very reluctantly, Chekhov felt that he must withdraw from Suvorin. 'How do you explain that?' Kovlevsky asked him, concerning Suvorin's behaviour. 'As nothing else than complete lack of backbone in Suvorin. I do not know of a man more undecided, even in questions pertaining to his family.' Lack of backbone—moral weakness—of this kind is in an entirely different category from envy and malice. Suvorin was obviously a decent man: but he was not a hero. Chekhov was a hero.

Friday, September 3rd.   Read four stories of Chekhov today: 'Kashtanka', 'The Peasants', 'The Bishop', 'The Letter'. God! what a marvellous fellow he was! And what must he be like in the original, if he makes this effect in translation. I don't think there is any other writer who tells so much of the truth, or makes humanity so beautiful . . .

In reading 'The Peasants', I stumbled on this passage, underlined by Katherine.

> Whenever there is some one in a family who has long been ill, and hopelessly ill, there come painful moments when all timidly, secretly, at the bottom of their hearts long for his death. (p. 298.)

And beside it, in her writing, 'and even write poems . . .'

Last night as I was going to bed, I looked hard at her photograph—into her sad eyes, in the portrait taken at Mentone; and I said aloud to her: 'There's something always so sad in your eyes when I look at you—as though you had been let down. But I don't think I let you down.' Nor do I think it. But maybe another would think my finding of that underlining and that note was the answer.

But, alas, it is not true. And oddly I would rather it was true than that it wasn't. I would really rather I was cruel to her than she unjust to me—I verily believe. But it doesn't matter. But the truth (as I remember it) was that never at any moment did I desire that she should die. I thought of her sometimes as dead, or tried to, I tried, and utterly failed, to imagine what it would be like if she did die. But how could I help doing that? And as for 'writing poems about it'—that is cruel. But I suppose if I were in her place, I should be cruel, unjust, too. It's just *human*.

Thursday, September 9th. Tomorrow I set off for a week in S. Wales. I hope it sets me right. I am now heartily sick of feeling 75% below par. 'Goodnight, Trousers,' I said to Mary in her funny pyjamas. 'Goodnight, Bags!' she promptly replied; and Weg and Col were entranced.

With the coming of autumn, the house had settled back into its normal routine. My brother returned to his school; I was entered at another now, the Grammar School in Thetford, where I was to go every day by bicycle and then by train; Betty's elemental rages were unleashed as of old.

14

Hopes and Fears

Miles and years away now, I look out of my window as I write and the cherry tree, after the endless winter, has burst into blossom. Never more lovely. Tight clusters of snow flowers crowd the black branches and swing gently against the blue spring sky.

Four hundred miles away as the crow flies and almost forty years. The invisible thread of memory trembles, plunges into darkness, a darkness of the soul that seemingly no human can uncover. Voices cry from the past. But how can they be heard from those depths where the being foundered, struggling desperately to breathe, to understand, to survive?

Down in the shadows agonies long motionless would move like giant bats. They would come through my window at Larling and crash blindly against the wall on heavy leathern wings, squeaking their hideous language of fear. Then I would sleep under the bedclothes, my head buried deep.

'The child will smother!' Betty said.

'I should leave her alone. She'll be all right,' came my father's voice. Wise.

'Leave her alone.' Again my father's voice, weary, sighing at Betty's anger the following morning.

I stared at him, mutely willing him to stop, for this could only goad her to greater fury.

Too late, too late. The fatal words 'leave her alone' bounced, cruelly innocent, onto the breakfast table; the puffed wheat crackled in its pool of cold milk, the sugarless tea, a tepid beige lake, waited to be drunk on this summer's morning in the thatched summer-house.

My starched summer dress sat over my body, an uncomfortable

cold tent chafing my neck and arms, its little green bells showered on the white cotton so recently fallen from the dressmaker's blue hands, trembling, too, with cold.

'Aow yes, aow ye-es,' Miss Reynolds' lips moved, holding her spare pins, her mirror tipped just so as I stood in her little front room, very still, very straight, hardly breathing. My dark straight hair and dark eyes, the thin goose-flesh arms, talked from the mirror of an asiatic ugliness, of a non-belonging. A statement of fact as inevitable as everything else. Brown when I should have been strawberries and cream.

'Blue, Miss Reynolds?' exclaimed Betty, patting her hair, glancing in the mirror at herself. 'Oh, not for Weg. She can't wear blue.'

'Aow? No, ma'am.'

Blue of the azure summer skies of dreams, blue of my sister's beautiful eyes, blue of Col's sailing boat the *Jolly Roger*, blue of our first glimpses of the sea.

And there in front of me my bare legs with the grazed knees down to the sensible brown sandals.

'A large hem, Miss Reynolds. It can be let down next year.'

'Aow yes.'

I was turned round. Snip, snip went the steel scissors. The sleeve was 'placed'.

'Naow, Mrs Murry, haow many buttons would yew like?'

The starched frock with the correct number of buttons braved countless washdays, as I sat shivering in the summer-house, the home of sleepy spiders and wood-lice and earwigs, of discarded golf clubs and the croquet set in its wooden box, where my father used to work sometimes at a teak garden table and even try to teach me algebra.

'Now, a train goes through a tunnel at x miles an hour.'

Silence.

'And it meets another train,' here he stood his pencil up on end: 'At this point.'

'Yes, Dadda.'

'Now . . .'

And the voice would go on, rather tired and sad and full of patience.

'Are you quite sure you understand?'

'Yes, Dadda.' But it was all beyond me. I could not get enthusiastic over the trains and my desire was merely not to upset him overmuch by being such a dunce. It was not his fault. He had to be spared. I would never be any good anyway, so I might as well be practical about it and wait while the magical equations filled the page and my homework was done for me. That I would flounder even more deeply in a mass of incomprehensible matter was obvious. But the thing was to get through it all somehow. I was panic-stricken yet somehow resigned. Over the dewy lawn my eyes would wander to a blackbird digging for a worm.

'Now we'll try this one.' My father's voice from a long way off: '$x + y = \ldots$'

It faded. The blackbird dug and wrestled and hauled up the worm.

Cobweb nets glistened exquisitely over the fresh grass.

'Now is that *quite* clear?'

'Yes, Dadda. Thank you, Dadda.' How sad he would be if he knew just how hopeless I was. He was so innocent, he seemed to believe me when I said I understood. He even thought I was capable of understanding. He was a god upon the Olympian heights with knowledge enormous. And I was like a limb deprived of blood. I had come from the past. Which past? It was unknown to me. Dimly two dark ladies held the key. They looked out from their photographs. They held me in check by what I sensed was their hostility and refusal of me, a refusal irreversible because wrapped in death.

'Now, is that quite clear?'

'Yes, Dadda,' I lied.

'She's a liar!' The accusing finger of Betty, the woman who wore the flesh and blood of life, trembled in anger.

'Forgive me! Forgive me!'

I clung to her, put my arms about her neck, shaking with sobs. But there was no forgiveness, nothing could wash me, cleanse me of what I was. I had been conceived in the past. There was no possibility of forgiveness for that.

'She's a liar—a liar and a thief!' cried Betty.

My father lifted his head from his work and stared vaguely, uncomprehending.

'Oh yes she is,' she shouted. '*Your* daughter!'

'Now, please . . .'

If only he had said sternly, 'Then I will punish her!' But no. The 'now, please' was the worst possible thing he could say.

Moreover he went from bad to worse and sighed: 'Leave her alone, now.'

And Betty was right. I was both a liar *and* a thief. I had sat with my father on my school train when he came back from London, peering anxiously into that white face, adoring the man whose frail form, clothed in grey, his London attire, huddled in the carriage corner, sitting the eight precious miles with him until the last landmark where I would go back to the school carriages and get out innocently while Betty waited on the platform to drive him home. I would pretend I had not seen him. To perfection, doubtless.

As for thieving, I began with a sixpence here and there, hiding them in the Shakespeare bedhead. But that was only a beginning.

'Your precious daughter!'

*   *   *

The great house at Larling turns in memory on its own axis. As if I were a conjurer now. North, south, east or west: for me to choose. Which entry? Which garden? And each entry, each garden has its own wealth, not to be despoiled but known, shared, opened to the light.

I knew the fens where Col used to fish for dace and come back smelling of earthy water, where king-cups and wild forget-me-nots and cuckoo flowers were flung by an invisible arm in wondrous profusion, and the dragonfly darted above the little wooden planks that served as bridges over the swamps; when the cuckoo called over the years, his notes echoing to and fro over the span of my life-time and all the life-times of those who heard him as I did. In the blue sky a white cloud appeared and took you unawares. Between the sprouting hedges I would cycle up the hill from the school train as it puffed its own white clouds and disappeared beyond a ragged mass of trees frilled with ivy.

My cardboard school case I hooked somehow onto the brake-bar. The front mudguard rattled: I had forgotten to give it a kick before leaving the station to wedge it into its cock-eyed position of silence.

'Hail to thee, blithe spirit!'

I gave it the requisite bang with my foot and wobbled almost to a standstill.

Two yellow-hammers frolicked in the hedge, darting in and out and up and down in breathtaking flashes. The fields rolled softly down towards Larling Ford and the Angel Inn and the Post Office, and above them, higher and higher, the lark—not Shelley's, no one's, yet *the* lark that sends its message of joy direct to the heart, distilled, immediate, wordless.

I pushed my foot down hard upon the pedal, crossed the turn-pike and free-wheeled down the hill on the other side.

The vice closed as I turned up the long drive and held my heart in a stillness that allowed no breath.

The lark had sunk into its secret nest, the fields into long shadows. I walked the last, slow, reluctant steps into the house and up the back stairs.

'Rue! What's the matter?'

Ruby was sitting on the edge of her bed, her face so swollen and red as to be scarcely recognisable.

'Rue!'

Huge hiccoughs rose noisily, heaving and plunging her shoulders on an ocean of grief.

'Rue!' I put my arms round her, coaxing, 'Come on Rue, tell us!'

Her sodden handkerchief was screwed up in a ball in her hand. On the dressing-table were brown wire curlers with bits of hair on them screwed into grotesque shapes, and safety-pins from the bibs of her afternoon aprons.

'*She's* been in a bad mood. Is that it?'

More hiccoughs ending in long shudders.

'Don't you mind her, Rue.'

'On and on she's been at me—all day.'

The handkerchief ball unrolled.

'But why? What have you done?'

'First thing she started at me. Said them plates were greasy. Put her finger over them. Said she could see the grease. *Thick* with it, she said.'

Ruby's head was bent down showing her black wiry hair with its frizzed ends dotted with scurf. I thought of the oval papier-mâché basins in the scullery full of cloudy hot soda water, her hands, scarlet and cracked, fishing up the plates from the rinse water with a knife and stretching up to the wooden rack; her voice thrilling with emotion as she described the latest film she had seen on her half-day:

'And then as she was lying there dying . . .'

'Yes, yes? Oh go on, Rue, hurry up!'

'You polish them glasses, then!'

'Yes, yes!' The glasses are polished brilliant as can be, the last bit of fluff puffed off.

'As she was lying there . . . dying . . . the window opens . . . and in walks Rod (that's Clark, of course)!'

'But how can he walk through the window?'

'They were big windows. You know, like the drawing-room ones. And there were curtains all over and all round her bed and you could see them moving.' (She shudders.)

'Go on.'

'And he bends over her and he picks her up, *bodily*—in his arms.' Her voice thrills dramatically.

'And then?'

'Then she falls back . . . dead!'

'Oh, Rue! Did you cry?'

'Me an' Vi did. Terrible . . . It was a *lovely* picture!'

Now, up in her room with its distinctive frowsty smell mixed with 'Evening in Paris'—different from what we had, fascinating in its difference—all I could say was:

'Never you mind, Rue. You've got us—hasn't she, Mêh?'

My little sister was standing in the doorway, solemnly watching us with her enormous blue eyes swept with the long dark lashes. Silent.

'If it weren't for you children an' por Mr Murry I'd 'ave given in me notice years ago.'

'I'll tell you what, Rue. Let's go for a picnic tomorrow. Look! It's going to be fine. "Red sky at night shepherd's delight".'

Effectively, through her window overlooking the walled garden, the sun was sinking in fire, shafts of gold streaming into the room with dancing particles of gold dust in radiant suspension.

I hugged her.

'We'll make egg-sandwiches, and buns—you know, your special ones—and we'll take some ginger pop.'

Small and plump, her bandy legs dangled over the side of the bed with not even the tips of her shoes touching the floor-boards.

She nodded, blew her nose loudly, comforted.

We went downstairs into the kitchen. Bodge, before going home, popped his head round the door, his cap in one hand and signs of baldness revealed.

'Well I never!'

'Now none o' your cheek, Cyril!'

'If that ain't our little girl.' He winked, and on the door post his thick, gentle hand hovered.

'You wipe them boots!' Ruby remonstrated.

'Oho, givin' orders, are we? Her hubby'd better look out!'

'Garn, Cyril! 'Ere, take that ter sweeten yer!'

Bodge came in, stood at the table, stirred his tea and delicately lowered the spoon back into the saucer.

Minutes later there came the familiar cackle of a hen that has just laid an egg. Ruby had recovered her spirits.

The back door closed softly and Bodge lifted his leg over his cycle and set off steadily for home.

*   *   *

It was about this time that my father patiently embarked upon Betty's education: he set her to copy one of Keats' Odes. He hoped to improve her crooked, often unintelligible handwriting and at the same time, perhaps, to sow the seeds in her of an awareness of his favourite poet.

I can see now the pathos of their endeavours when Betty made a short-lived effort with the 'Ode to Autumn'. I was far from despising Betty with her copy-book: on the contrary, I rather envied her ensconced in the drawing-room with poetry, while I had been sent to the scullery to wash my school blouses.

At his desk my father was involved in Milton and Wordsworth for *Heaven—and Earth*. But his health, which he had felt lately to be '75% below par', could take the strain of domestic scenes and over-work no longer. Paralysis in one leg had doubtless set in when I noticed his slight limp as we walked together to the little church for the Sunday service:

?1937.   A lovely day, at any rate after noon. In the morning I
went to Communion. Perhaps it was a mistake. Anyhow, I felt
languid and tired and inclined rather to criticise the parson's
stupid and pretentious reading of the service than disposed to
meditate. As Katherine said, It is hard to be humble: one *is*
always 'preening oneself'. All the same, I do think it preposter-
ous, if no worse, that the parson should make nonsense of parts
of the service.

'O Lord and heavenly Father, we thy humble servants
entirely—desire thy fatherly goodness . . .'

'Most humbly beseeching thee to grant that . . . we and thy
whole Church may obtain remission—of our sins and all other
benefits of his passion.'

This last one was indeed maddening; not a bit funny and
delightful like Farmer Carter's 'First Epistle of General St
Peter'.

I don't know what is the minimum one ought to require of a
parson these days; but I do feel that he ought not to get in the
way of meditation. Still, that doesn't alter the fact that it was
my fault. How I hate the measly hymns, too, with only a
half-dozen to sing them!

Wednesday, October 13th.   I gave Betty her first—or my
first—writing lesson this morning. It was touch and go: she
had a bad pen, and it went badly, so she broke out into blame of
the copy I had made for her. Then I lent her my pen, and things
began to go better, until by the end she was very happy, and
trying very hard. I was very much moved by the tears in her
eyes, when she said: 'I think, if you had given me more
attention, when we were first married, things would have been
much happier.' But, as I said, in those days I should have been
frightened of offending her by suggesting that I should give her
lessons in writing and spelling. It's plain enough, *now*, that I
shouldn't have done. As a matter of fact, she made quite
remarkable progress in a few minutes, writing her name quite
differently. Her fingers are simply unused to writing: which she
has avoided because it suggested her inferiority. This inferiority, I believe, isn't real. She can do all these things: but
somehow, by some malign accident, her childish love was

repulsed. She was made to feel she was inferior: and so she neglected herself—to the extent of taking a perverse delight in being ignorant.

Anyway, at the end of the lesson I felt I had had a revelation into Betty's simple soul such as I had never had before: and it overwhelmed me for a moment—the pathos and beauty of it.

What a magnificent *Englishman* John Milton was! Not even Shakespeare has said quite such superb things—such insolently confident things—about England. Those in *Areopagitica* are familiar to me: but these two, from the preface of the *Doctrine of Divorce*, were new. 'Let not England forget her precedence of teaching nations how to live'; 'our wanted prerogative, of being the first asserters in every great vindication'. On the fag and degenerate end of that spirit we are living today.

Saturday, November 6th.   I had better record that in Glasgow I found that my right leg right up to the pelvis would go cramped and numb after I had walked a hundred yards or so: and this has continued ever since. I hope it's not the *vaunt-courier* of some sort of paralysis. In the last two years—and increasingly in the last year—I have noticed a definite narrowing of my physical circle, so to speak. I can't do things I used to do, and I cease to try to do them. (The first sign of my disease.)*

Thursday, November 12th.   From T.† a curious letter describing an encounter with a 'psychic' who was violently perturbed by T.'s obligations to 'John and David'. (To be remembered that at that very moment, when, I believe, the child was conceived, or begotten, I was filled with a sense of fulfilling D.H.L.—that he was (in some way) corporeally existent in me at that moment: that this was the motive of my telling Betty the next day that he was to be called David.)‡

Thursday, November 18th.   I dipped into the *Areopagitica* again. But how to convey that a man's very wrongness is the condition of his superb rightness—and that's a poor way of

---

* This note was made at a later date and refers to Burger's Disease.
† Winifred Trimby, whom we called Trim.
‡ A note added later.

putting it? That the real universe *must* always be the particular.
It is *so* plain to me: so evidently the truth of Life: yet I cannot
formulate it even to myself. And then I read Oliver's speech to
the Barebones Parliament—fit counterpart to the *Areopagitica*: with something in it—tenderness: the tenderness of a
strong man—which even the *Areopagitica* has not got. But
those two utterances together—if they will not move a *man*,
what will?

Tuesday, December 7th.   Yesterday, I read Herbert Read's
Wordsworth—an interesting and well-written book with
the common failing of exaggerating a partial truth into the
whole. The whole and sufficient cause of Wordsworth's poetic
decline is his unresolved conflict about Annette Vallon. I
simply cannot see *how* this can be made to work. Wordsworth's absolute optimum is 1798–1802; he is still first-rate
until 1807 (and we can account for any relative decline by his
work on the *Prelude*). It is somewhere between 1807 and 1815
that the real poetic decline begins. Now it may be, possibly,
that W. had more or less promised Annette and *himself* that he
would marry her when the war was over: and that his inward
spring broke when he realised that he was not going to do
so—when, in fact, on October 4, 1802, he married Mary
Hutchinson instead. I have a notion that H.R. is pretty well on
the spot at this point: but there are two strands, both involved
in his marrying of Mary Hutchinson—1) the hypothetical
breach of faith with Annette and 2) the much more real breach
of some subtle relation with Dorothy. And 3) the effect on the
relation with Coleridge seems to have been instant.
    The clue appears to lie rather in the break-up of this extra-
ordinarily subtle threefold relation between W.W., D.W., and
S.T.C. Annette and Mary being, as it were, the heterosexual
thread of the norm. It is the intricate condition of the space
between one heterosexual relation and the other that is the
condition of the great work: when the sexual libido of a
passionate man was sublimated in a very extraordinary way in
a unique relation between three people of genius—the sort of
relation I can dimly conceive as occurring between Lawrence,
Katherine and me—reckoning me, merely *ad hoc*, as a genius. I

think the truth lies somewhere about here. I *must* some day write a real book on W.W.

*   *   *

It was soon to be Christmas. With holly tucked above the pictures and little bowls of coloured chocolates prepared for the table. It would not snow, but Bodge had dug up our Christmas tree and we had put on the tinsel and the shiny balls, the silver bell, the star and the candles. It stood grandly in the corner by the bay window. Christmas was like a dream island, when time stops, a magic moment.

> 'Good King Wenceslas last looked out
> On the feast of Stephen . . .'

Col and I, with Mêh, went round carol singing. Col sang well. I only managed to keep up and chime in without getting too flat. Mêh dutifully brought up the rear. We went round to our own front door, and began:
'One, two, three!' A deep breath: 'Good King Wenceslas . . .'
When we had got through there was much whispering:
'When Shepherds watched their flocks?'
'No, "The First Noël".'
Here we quavered a bit:

> 'The-e fir'st No-o-ël
> The-e angel did say . . .'

We rattled a cocoa tin with a few pennies in it, waiting expectantly, a little fearfully. Excited.
'It's a bad day today, we shouldn't have tried,' we whispered.
'Yes, but it's *Christmas*,' said one of us, encouraged in our stout-heartedness by the surrounding dark. Indeed, there was not a star in sight.
The hall light went on. We could see it under the door. And hear footsteps coming along through the glass door, over the matting. The bolts were sliding.
'The-e fir-st No-o-ël,' Col started up vigorously. Rattle, rattle went the tin.
'Alms for the poor carol singers!' I shouted from the safety of outside.

'Darlin', it's the children!' shouted Betty, her light brown hair reflected in the golden pool of light as her white face retreated from peering glumly into the dark and her shapely legs strode stiffly back towards the study.

We rattled the cocoa tin even louder.

She came back with a few coins and grudgingly dropped them in.

'That's enough. Now go away. Leave me in peace.'

'Good King Wenceslas . . .'

'Thank'ee, thank'ee, ma'am.' One of us affected an elaborate bow enfolded by the gentle night.

> '. . . When the snow lay round about
> Deep and crisp and even.
> Brightly shone the moon that night,
> Though the frost was cru-el . . .'

We moved down the gravel drive beyond the laurels, toeing the delightful dark. Together. Behind us the house, with the door tight shut, loomed larger than life, throttling life. We laughed and broke into a trot, now over the flints and the ruts of the long drive beneath the beech trees until we reached the tarred road and could thud smoothly along to the Hewetsons' bungalow. To a more welcoming door.

And this is how my father remembered that Christmas:

Sunday, December 26th, 1937.   Yesterday, Christmas morning, I was tired and had my breakfast in bed. I got up at a quarter to nine and sat for some minutes in my study in my dressing gown . . . I hurried off to Christmas Communion: and this sank deeper into my heart perhaps than ever before:

Almighty God, our heavenly Father, who of thy tender mercy didst give thy only son, Jesus Christ, to suffer death upon the Cross for our redemption; who made there (by his one oblation of himself once offered) a full, perfect and sufficient sacrifice, oblation and satisfaction for the sins of the world . . .

15

Overtones of War

I write and pause again, staring at the cherry tree outside my window, where clusters of little hard green fruits are forming; the late morning glows blue and green and gold, and a blue-bottle bangs against the pane and flies away. I think of the garden of my childhood, although cherries did not do well there.

But the peaches and nectarines clung to the red brick walls and Bodge, with a rabbit's tail on the end of a stick, touched their deep pink flowers like a magician with his wand.

'What's your favourite rose, Bodge?'

'Ah . . . Well, it must be "Crimson Glory". She's a beauty.'

His braces were hanging over his thighs in loops. His boots with their homely rounded toes sank into the soft earth. 'She'll be around June time. Right lovely she is.'

'Bodge . . .'

'Anything up, Bodgie?' He went on tickling the blossoms one by one with the white rabbit's tail.

'Did you know? *She* might be going away?'

'Oh? You don't say so!'

'Yes. I wish she'd go on another. On a cruise, I mean. To Bermuda again or somewhere.'

'Ah. Is that so, now!'

'So we'll be just us: you and Rue and us—and Dadda, of course.'

At that moment there were cries from the house and shouts. Then Mary's voice:

'Mummy! Mummy! Don't, Mummy!' mounting to a wail.

'There goes the Missus,' sighed Bodge. 'On again.'

The earth along the path edge glittered fresh. The box hedge was putting forth new leaves.

'When . . .?' but my voice caught now. 'When . . . are you going to plant out the snap-dragons?'

'Few days from now. Depending.'

'De . . . depending on what?'

There was a scream, a crash, the tinkle of broken glass.

'My word! Oh dear, oh dear!' The rabbit's tail rejoined the bunch of bass in the greenhouse. Bodge slipped his braces back over his shoulders. His blue eyes clouded. I could see his hands tremble slightly.

'It's Dadda, Bodge. D'you think he's all right?'

'Better'd go in and see. Slip round the back. I'll go to the kitchen. Jus' natural like. Now you mind you. She's real bad today.'

Sliding my hand over the books I went into the hall. The drawing-room door was ajar but no one was inside. The study door was shut, its black shiny knob glistening. I turned it gently and peered round. My father was seated at his desk. He had not heard me. I tiptoed over to him and put my hand over his shoulder.

'Are you all right, Dadda?' I whispered. His bowed head and the extreme stillness of his posture disturbed me.

'Dadda . . . Dadda . . .'

Then I looked down and on the pink blotting paper saw splashed tears. They were rolling down his cheeks. In the corner of the pad a heart had been drawn with an arrow through it, with the words: 'KM/JM—The bes' of all'. It had remained there as Katherine Mansfield had left it—for how many years?

My father obviously had not expected me then. And there I was, witnessing something so private.

I stood there speechless, my hand still resting on his shoulder. In an egg-cup were buttercups and birds-eye, the 'bunch' that Mêh had brought in for his desk.

Away in the distance a cuckoo called, now insistent, now fading into the general choir of birds.

I stood and shared his grief. Although I did not perhaps know its deepest source, I was aware simply that he had been tried beyond endurance; my heart hardened to bitterness against the woman who had done this, and it rode side by side with my fear of her.

I waited, not daring to move while the grief spent itself, motionless behind the motionless head. Then finally he said, 'Ah, darling,' with a kind of short laugh. 'We're in a pretty fix!'

'It will be all right, Dadda.' I let my cheek rest against the fine softness of his thinning hair with its smell of soap and tobacco.

But something had come to an end, something had snapped. I did not know what it was. Merely sensed it: a pall of doom.

Suddenly the door opened and Betty entered holding a book in her hand—it was one of my father's diaries—he was notoriously careless of his things, rarely putting away his papers, often losing them. She looked crazed. Her face was white. The lines between nose and mouth were deep. Her pale blue eyes were expressionless yet full of frenzy, as if the passion itself was soul-less.

She was possessed of superhuman strength. I could feel the old familiar surge of terror mounting my legs to my knees.

Like a bird of prey whose wings quiver, displacing the air in waves of imminent destruction, the hovering menace filled the room.

And my father had given her poetry to copy, to improve her handwriting; the words in their rich serenity seemed ludicrously inappropriate now:

Season of mists and mellow fruitfulness . . .

The pen had crawled over the page like a drunken spider.

At this moment her anger was whipped to paroxysm by my father's aura of remoteness; he sat there, shut away within himself, impregnable. She towered above him, shaking, the very flesh on her arms quivering.

'Get out, woman, get out of here and let me work!'

But this only goaded her the more. A further stream of obscenities was followed by blows. The old terror lest she kill him made me strong with desperation.

It was not the end of the battle. There was in fact no end, only a lull. The reason why she gave up and walked out was within herself, the ebb and flow of hysteria that was beyond reason.

But still one has to live. When one is young, however much one truly longs for death, the passion for life is deep and strong: it rises like the sap in a young tree, as inevitably; it rises through the veins, captious and heady, as though it came from the earth itself; up through the soles of one's feet, giving them invisible wings, up and up with a strange music of no note, a harmony one can feel but cannot express, until it issues from all the tips of one's being, with such a power as to hold all else in abeyance. Such brilliance! Such glory!

Springtime. I cycled down the hills headlong, sometimes holding my breath for as long as possible. If I got to such a tree without breathing . . . if . . . if . . . then I'd win. Win what? What race? What ambition was mine?

            *   *   *

The smocked lady visitors in their flat sandals, who had come to Larling for the Adelphi Summer School or on other occasions, to meet and converse with their *great man*, appeared for the last time that summer and left, startled out of their folksy vegetarianism, their timid adoration of my father, by Betty's unique brand of expeditiousness. From their country cottages, their suburban houses, their town flats, they were so innocent of the real world, grim and beautiful, that was Larling. How could it have been otherwise: they in their little dream worlds of Art, Beauty, Charity, Love? At Larling such notions just did not fit. It was a wonder if these acquaintances lasted a week. They left tearfully. We, the children, bade them goodbye with mild interest and regret. It was a pity. In their presence was a certain *piment*, and they directed Betty's violence to other channels and away from us.

The men usually lasted longer. Indeed, sometimes they had a special flat assigned them, over the 'bottle-room' which was full of old jam-jars and empty bottles and had a winey, cobwebby, mildewy smell. Up a flight of wooden stairs, on each side, were two little rooms that looked out westwards over the herbaceous border and the path leading through the gate to the beech avenue and the walled garden.

Sometimes my father was rather like a friendly lion. Would he roar or just open his mouth with a yawn and shut it again?

'What are you thinking about, Dadda?'

He would wink and reply: 'Well . . . just nothing. No—' he would eye us wickedly as if he'd been bluffing the world, 'not a thought, not a single thought!'

At other times he would pace the lawn with Sir Richard Rees or some other intrepid visitor, discussing politics. Strange words like 'bourgeois', 'bolshevism', 'totalitarian', used to float upon our ears.

I did not understand. Yet understood. My father was always right—there was no question. Why did the others not understand and accept it? Why couldn't they stop arguing? All those discussions, so long, what was the point when he was right anyway?

A young man came and did a drawing on a piece of paper. It looked like a few sticks joined here and there but never crossing.

'What is that?' he asked.

My father looked a moment then said, 'It's sex. Man—Woman. Of course.' Why, of course! Naturally! He knew.

The young man nodded. How extraordinary, when no one else could answer! The young man was a clever psychiatrist. Extraordinary? Silly young man! I thought, how did he not know my father knew? How remarkably obtuse people could be! Perhaps it came from the pale podginess of the young man's round face and small eyes blinking behind the spectacles.

Then there was Mr R. Whether he was insane on arrival or whether we children and Betty had driven him to this pitch, we never knew. In the middle of the night he came from his bedroom and stood at the top of the stairs announcing loud and plain that he was 'going through the golden gates'.

Mr R. left next morning and was never seen again, but doubtless the poor man had been sorely tried for many days: Betty did not 'take to him'. He was one of those 'intellectuals'; she could not abide them. She would get rid of them 'in a good spring-clean', along with 'old Lawrence's slippers' (his beaded moccasins), his paintings and Katherine's old belongings. They made such a clutter in the bedroom cupboard where my mother's ashes, which my father had forgotten to scatter, still lay wrapped up in a brown paper parcel. The paintings were thrown away, lost to posterity, like so much else.

Betty was lonely. She had no friends. No woman with whom she could exchange recipes or share children, *parler chiffons* and laugh with, trouncing the men-folk when they were in the way.

But for us children there was something strange and magical about a visitor hailing from the bathroom in the morning, freshly shaved and smelling quite different. He could have come from the moon or Mars in his unfamiliar dressing-gown. We gazed as he disappeared into his flat, gazed again as he reappeared, spruced and ready for breakfast.

Sir Richard Rees was one of these. He was kind, good-humoured, gentle, well-bred, with that natural breeding beyond caste. His love for my father was manifest, his quiet tolerance of Betty and affection for her enduring. He lived in the flat, off and on, for many months. We hardly ever entered: it was forbidden territory, remote, rather awe-inspiring. There was a soft quietness about it, a gentle authority. The nearest we would get would be to tap on the door with a 'Surrichard, lunch is ready'. Perhaps we would peep round, eyeing his desk and papers. But he was wise and knew where to draw a kind yet firm line with us.

We learned that he had been in Spain, driving an ambulance, and had not had his boots off for more than *six weeks*, that *grass grew in them*. We were deeply impressed.

'Surrichard' went on a voyage to the East and brought us back presents. Little bowls of burnished lacquer for Col and a necklace of jade elephants for me. They ran their cool, almost transparent course round my neck. I put them away in cotton-wool for best, fingering every now and then each lifted trunk, each dividing bead.

One day, when I was in Betty's bedroom, I saw them on her dressing-table, broken. I dared not say a word. I just glanced at them as they lay carelessly strewn there and pretended not to notice or, if I noticed, not to mind.

Strange how tiny things remain, blotting out the big. I can still see them. Some had rolled down onto the floor and stuck between the dark, varnished floorboards . . .

*   *   *

In 1937 my father had joined the Peace Pledge Union along with Richard Rees, George Orwell, Aldous Huxley and many others. Later he was to edit its paper, *Peace News*. Towards the end of that year, although critical of the Church establishment, he contemplated taking Orders and joined a group of religious and social thinkers which included A. R. Vidler, Karl Mannheim and T. S. Eliot. They met to exchange ideas and hoped to influence the ecclesiastical hierarchy. It was called the *Moot*; to us children my father would teasingly call it the 'Toom', which conjured up odd visions of his doings . . .

Especially impressed by the refugee Mannheim, he would say that until we in England have known what it is to be spied upon by the secret police or have worked under a terror, we cannot be completely realistic.*

In spite of the growing pain in his leg, he went on writing and addressing meetings. Meanwhile, the only effect his religion and pacifism had on Betty was to make her jeer. After one of their terrible rows my father was driven into a strange state which was nearer to mysticism than anything:

January 3rd?, 1938.   Now I copy a note I made in the train this morning. 'How strange this morning at Harling Road Station was the sense of Physical rebirth after travail, and death. I said to myself aloud on the platform: "I'm a dead man", almost unconsciously, and at the same moment experienced the joy, thin, unsubstantial, transparent, of being in a new physical world. The station roof was, as it were, the geometrical "idea" of itself—a shape more real than materiality—and the railway lines seemed to vibrate. It was the condition which Lawrence so magically conveys in *The Man Who Had Died*.

'Strange, too, the *sudden* feeling last night, when I had gone down to the drawing-room in a condition of blank and utter despair ("No life, no life!")—the sudden feeling that came over me after talking with Richard,† that the crisis was "all over" —a miraculous and almost joyful calm. Almost a certainty that love *must* prevail, because there was no other way. But that's not accurate: just an utterly unexpected, unhoped for change —a breath of wind from the warm South—from death and despair to life and joy. I don't know, but probably Richard's love (of me *and* Betty) had much to do with it.'

But what in such a condition does hanging on to Christ *mean*? Nothing. There is nothing, nobody, to hang on to. But that also may be hanging on to Christ. My God, my God, why hast thou forsaken me?

Monday, January 24th.   A spring day: Mary brought me in a little bowl of primroses! Richard‡ was down for the weekend. Of course, I take him for granted, and it's only at intervals that I

* Conversation with F. A. Lea.
† Sir Richard Rees.
‡ Richard Murry.

become fully conscious of how much nearer to me, in feeling, idea and ideal, he is than any other man. I have known it a long while now, and for certain ever since we worked on the Centre together: but yesterday and this morning was one of the rare occasions when it became an immediate and overbrimming feeling. Our ideals are now, so far as I can tell, identical: our plan, whether we fully accomplish it or not is gradually and modestly to establish a new centre of community life, in some sort of natural harmony with existing village life—to print works expressive of the idea—my proposed commentary on Blake's *Milton*; to live simply; to run 'a school'; to keep the solid foundation of family life; to have a definite and avowed Christian basis for it all. I am, if possible, to become the village parson, he the artist and craftsman. It is a thing, at any rate, which we can work at to the end of our lives, and feel we have done something. But for the present we must mark time (if 'marking time' is a fair phrase for either of us at any period). He has to concentrate on his painting for a year; I have to concentrate on 1) pulling *The Adelphi* through and 2) preparing for taking orders.

Yes, I think this sense of total agreement with Richard has *finally* clinched my purpose of taking orders. It has now become wholly natural—as the leaves to a tree. Now, *no* impatience! Things are happening fast enough, in all conscience.

Sunday, January 30th.   That same morning was Mary's birthday (6). I knew all about it the night before, but in the morning I had forgotten it. As usual, we went into the bathroom together, and I began to shave. Suddenly, I was aware of her standing still against the *old* door, with her head bent, and her long eyelashes conspicuous. Then she said: 'Dadda! you *needn't think* I'm only five!' My heart ached, and I hugged her. Then we had a dance together round the bathroom, singing 'Many happy returns of the day—many happy returns of the day'. And so it was all forgiven and forgotten.

Tuesday, February 15th.   Betty and I are reading aloud in the evenings Max's *A Subaltern on the Somme*: it's very good, one of the very best of the war-books. It awakens in me the old feeling that to balance my account with God I shall have to be killed—only on the anti-war side. I think that now, with God's help, I shall be able to face it; but there's no doubt that the effort to face it—to keep my head turned in that direction —has turned me into the complete Christian. By which I don't mean a believer in a glorious resurrection. I am afraid that's something in which I shall never be able to believe. It's not important enough to *believe* in. What I am trying to say there is that all necessary beliefs, all true beliefs, are ultimately enforced upon a man who submits to life, and belief in a glorious resurrection is not among them.

Yet, in a sense, it is: that real and abiding existence of Jesus, (of Keats, of Blake, of Lawrence, in a lesser degree) is not merely a subjective thing: it is something more—something objective. But what I really mean by that I cannot say, nor can I ever hope to discover the mode of that objective eternality . . .

Thursday, February 17th.   The last four days have been days of crisis in Austria, and the grip of Nazi Germany upon that country has increased. To my foreboding imagination it seems like the disappearance of another—and historically one of the greatest—citadels of European civilisation. Vienna that repelled the Turk 250 years ago now surrenders to German barbarism. Yet perhaps there is also a gleam of salvation in it: one more nucleus of Christian resistance taken into the Nazi barbarism. But I am afraid of some sinister bargain between the Vatican and Hitler and Mussolini. The Vatican will sacrifice Austria and the South-German Catholics to regain Spain. Germany, allowed to absorb Austria, will be benevolent towards Mussolini's designs on Spain. I don't know. Does anybody know? But assuredly the future looks grimmer and grimmer.

Saturday, February 19th.   . . . Hitler's Austrian coup means the last flicker of the Holy Roman Empire. *Actum est.* The third Reich is in being, conjured up by an Austrian house-painter who hated and hates the very notion of the Holy Roman Empire. 'Where the carcase is, there will be the eagles gathered together'—the vultures, the carrion-eagles of Hitlerism. Even

the last *Prussian* virtue gone in the process. It is an end (I verily
believe) of *Roman* Catholicism. Now only the Catholic Church
of Christ. Catholicism and Christ; Christ not Rome the centre
of Catholicism. Is it a vision or a waking dream?

＊   ＊   ＊

My mind follows the ellipse of time further back to Ruby's cackling
laugh as she pushes the pram down the drive, with Mêh sitting in it
looking out at the world with her huge blue eyes, and Col and I
trotting alongside—we were growing taller than Ruby. She
waddled sturdily along the road on her bandy legs and we hung on
to the handlebars. 'Don't drag like that!' she would say. We would
remember for a while, then hang on again.

The pram was old and sagged rather at the bottom. A far cry from
the fashionable landaus and lace-trimmed baby boats of other
proud owners. It rattled and shook its way past the fens and
squeaked over the wooden ford bridge.

The little girl grew out of the pram and she was very beautiful, so
fair, so slim, so tall.

Why did Col leave me for her, I wondered bitterly as she followed
Col about and fetched and carried for him adoringly. Why was I left
out? Had not Col and I always shared everything? Why did he deny
me now?

I stood in the walled garden on my way back from school one day.
He was there.

'What shall we do, Col? Climb trees?'

He looked at me as from a distance, then disapprovingly down to
my stockinged legs.

'Whatever have you got on?'

'Why,' I stammered, blushing, 'I have to wear those now for
school. It's the uniform.'

'Oh . . .'

'Shall we? And make a house in the box-tree?'

He frowned, then shouted over his shoulder:

'Mêh! Come on, Mêh!' and ran away with his little sister trotting
happily after him.

I stood there. The horrid beige stockings wrinkled on my legs. An
era had passed. Something was over. I knew it on the instant. And
the white rose bush beside which I stood, *my* rose bush that Bodge

had given me, seemed to know, too. Where was I now? To whom could I belong?

'Mêh!' The intimacy of it, the binding exclusiveness with Mary waiting in round-eyed devotion. It was a beautiful thing, their relationship, and I stood outside, jealously, as if outside a fairy ring.

Yet sometimes it would expand and make room for me, as when we gave our theatrical performances in the box-rooms. I wrote a play called *Septimus's Revenge*. We acted it with fervour. Col did the lighting and the stage props, I the costumes and the make-up. Mêh had to learn her lines which she did not understand and, at times, neither did we. Ruby was roped in, too. There was much clashing of swords and sweeping of blanket cloaks, and explanatory asides to the guests when necessary. An interval with refreshments was allowed its full due. Aunt Doll and a brave young visitor fresh from Cambridge, Mr Frank Lea, with my father, Bodge and anyone else we could find, were the audience. When the play ended with, 'It was thy folly, Septimus!' Mr Lea was to note that no one could discover what Septimus's folly had been, but that all warmly applauded and my father was in fits of laughter. We were well pleased. Col's lights in the biscuit tins had worked, Mêh had been successfully prompted, the costumes made from old chair covers had had their effect . . .

Then there was the great hailstorm.

The wind shook the beech leaves, a bad, whirling wind, curling and tearing, breaking. The wind of a summer storm.

A roll of thunder sounded far off over Lumley's field. Then a flash of lightning zig-zagged, electric-blue in the sky. The black clouds rose up in black hills. My father had told us of a boy who had been killed by a stroke of lightning on the cricket pitch at his school, and I saw in my mind the stark, bare tree with its naked arms in our Church Meadow. In the distance Mrs Lumley hurried home under her old felt hat, the colour of earth itself, that she wore winter and summer alike.

Beneath the beech trees and chestnuts and round the corner up the cobbled yard I ran, in through the side door and upstairs to the nursery.

Bang! Bang, crash! Suddenly from the black sky hail started to fall.

Crash! came the sound of splintering glass from the skylight above the stairs. Col was rushing about excitedly with a pencil and pad, noting with wild triumph every pane of glass shattered by the hail.

My father was in bed pumping air round his legs which were stretched out beneath the shelf he had made to hang all the instruments.

'That makes seven in all from the skylight and twenty in the greenhouse!' said Col, adding to his list.

My father groaned.

'Two in the west room and there's nothing left at the top of the back stairs!'

My father groaned once more. Col rushed out again. Crash! Bang! His reporting was by no means finished.

'Twenty-seven in the greenhouse and two more in the skylight. That makes . . . let me see . . . twenty-seven plus seven plus two not counting the box-rooms . . .!'

'That'll do, old boy,' said my father faintly, 'I think it's blowing over now.'

But Col's final list was catastrophic.

'As big as golf-balls!' he cried gleefully as he leaped about the house. 'Look at that one, Dadda,' and he brought an enormous hailstone to my father in his hand.

When the storm was over and the last thunder had rolled away into the distance, my father did the rounds to assess the damage. It really was dreadful. Of the greenhouse little was left, the skylight was full of holes and all about outside trailed pathetic branches of green leaves in pools of water.

The blackbirds were sending out their loud clear notes, while all the other birds were hushed, and in the returned warmth there was a pungent smell above the nettle beds underneath Lumley's apple-trees.

Then the wood-pigeons started up, calling from tree to tree, and far away could be heard children's voices shouting and crying out and laughing as they came out from school: a music of sounds, a crowding of smells upon the tingling nostrils. Branches and broken flowers and petals floated in the muddy pools, and Bodge in his heavy boots tramped round the garden. With his cap on the back of his head he scratched his brow.

'Coo! Lor'! Lummy!' he said privately to us and, to my father,

choosing his words more carefully: 'Well, sir, I never saw the like
. . . I never did!' Then in a voice low with sympathy, 'And that's
going to cost a pretty penny, I'll be bound . . .'

My father smiled ruefully and continued his inspection with us
children at some distance, outwardly subdued but still seething with
excitement.

Then 'Sly Bye' and Lenny came to put in new panes. Up on the
ladder, in his white apron, creases round his twinkling eyes, 'Sly
Bye' would wink down at us . . .

           *   *   *

Even his rows with Betty could not vanquish my father's spirit.
After each of her paroxysms had burnt themselves out hope sprang
anew in him. Our home, at once so cruel and so beautiful, so
solid-looking and yet so fragile beside the unfolding drama of
Europe, touched him in fleeting moments with deepest joy.

This subtle alchemy of opposing experiences illuminated, I think,
his prophetic understanding at that time.

Monday, March 14th, 1938. On Saturday, Hitler advanced
with 50 or 100 thousand troops into Austria, and Austria is
now part of the German Reich. What might have taken a year
or two has been accomplished in two days! Whether it bodes
good or ill, who can say? The Anschluss itself was necessary
and inevitable: but because it has been accomplished in this
way it probably means a liberation of energy for evil . . .

Tuesday, April 12th. The *Aryan Path* has sent me a clumsy
little Indian reprint of a book: *Hind Swaraj, or Indian Home
Rule*, written by Gandhi in 1908. It is a truly remarkable little
book—a classic almost by the simple lucidity of its expression:
and certainly an epoch-making little book by the profundity of
its insight. A *great* little book, which I am very glad to have
read, and shall read again. A masterpiece of religion and
philosophy. Note particularly the novel insight of spiritual
genius in his little chapter on 'History'; also the historical
perspective of the East, in which European 'civilisation'
appears as an upstart of yesterday—and how prophetic it is
concerning the downfall of that 'civilisation'. There is room for

a deeply interesting comparison of Rousseau and Gandhi: Rousseau representing the Christian-European mind at its best.

Wednesday, April 13th. . . . But then I have twinges of conscience from the fact that I am so happy here at home just now. Today at tea-time, for example, there were only Betty and the three children and me—and a great deal of palaver in the kitchen; and the full, living, oh, so *ordinary* peace, was lovely. It seemed to me that I had never known anything like it, since Katherine and I were at Bandol in 1916, and even that was not quite so simple, quite so much in the simple stream of life. It is not so much a twinge of conscience as a twinge of fear that afflicts me. Shall I be required to surrender it all? Is it, can it be, *right* to be so happy while the world is like it is? And the answer is that, whether it is right or not, I cannot do otherwise. I cannot torment myself to order. I suppose I keep my mind as fixed as most men's on the underlying horror of 'this present world'; I have kept it fixed on it *more* than most men, and I do keep it so fixed. But, in spite of all, I am happy. I am doing what I can; it seems to me I can't do more. I have no *call* to forsake my family—far less a call to make my children miserable. Somehow, I feel that, if we are happy (as we are) the happiness has been paid for, and is legitimate. Anyway, I cannot help it. I can't just *make* myself miserable; and I'm certainly not going to try to.

Saturday, May 8th. . . . Yesterday I heard that I am to go into the Nursing Home tomorrow, Sunday. It's a queer fatality that this should happen just when the baby is going to be born —just when I hoped to have reached port after stormy seas. 'Whom the Lord loveth he chasteneth', and I could almost believe that the most foolish thing I ever did in my life was to speak above a whisper of my discovery of a loving God. That is, of course, 'childish'; but truly I am haunted by the fear that I shall not escape—that I shall have to surrender houses and lands and wife and *children*. It is that which hurts. And I want to plead for 15 years more: then Mary would be 21 and Weg and Col out in the world living their own lives. I hope and believe I should be absolutely content to go then. But before that, it would be *hard*: because I know that B. whom I love—and I know it because I love her—cannot do without me. Were she of a different make-up (in which case probably I should not have loved her) I should know that she was well able to look after the children; and I could fold up my tent like the Arab. As it is . . .

My father's next journal, which must have covered the rest of 1938 and into 1939, described, I suppose, his personal life in too dreadful a detail, for Betty destroyed it.

16

David

On 24th May, 1938, while my father was in the nursing home
having electrotherapy treatment on his legs, my brother David was
born. It happened early in the morning, before I had gone to school.
Betty called me to see him before he had been washed, but the
doctor, who had brought Mêh into the world six years before,
shocked to his small eyes, kept the bedroom door firmly locked.

When I came back in the evening I rushed upstairs to see the baby.
There had never been any doubt among us that it would be a boy
and named David.

He outstripped in beauty all I had imagined. I had always felt
dolls cheated by pretending to be alive with their eyes opening and
closing and the chill flush of their porcelain cheeks. Now here, at
last, was the real thing. With powder and pins, creams and eye-
wash, I cherished this babe perfect beyond all dreams.

Up in the nursery, with the click of knitting needles and the hum
of the sewing machine, the industry that summer was prodigious.
On sunny days David would sleep beneath a net in the Moses basket
under the branches of the weeping ash. There I would often have tea
beside him, with Ruby cackling a joke and Granny Burlingham
laughing so much that once she lost her false teeth in the grass . . .

My father in his radicalism was now finding it difficult to make a
living as a writer.

'Why don't you write stuff to make money?' Betty would say to
him.

'What would you propose, my dear?'

'A play. You could write that.'

'Do you like his books?' enquired Frank Lea, who recorded this
conversation.

'Good God, I never read *them*,' Betty replied.

Betty had got rid of Miss Watt and Frank was now my father's secretary. He was blessed with a liking for children and we found his presence in the household a definite 'plus factor'. He entered into our games with gusto and sometimes took us out in his old two-seater, jogging over the Norfolk countryside.

The international situation grew even more menacing. Hitler was now turning his attention to the Sudetens. At the end of September came the Munich crisis and, two months later, the International Brigades withdrew from Spain.

I attributed my father's pallor to these exterior events. But the electrotherapy had had no effect upon the paralysis in his legs. An operation was the only alternative if he were not to lose them altogether.

So in April of the following year he spent a month in hospital where he underwent a sympathectomy.

*   *   *

At school the chemistry formulae crowded upon the blackboard, pushed and squabbled, glided smooth, sat pretty only to be rubbed out into the chalk dust that filled the groove below. From behind the bunsen burner I stared stupidly, uncomprehending, shaking a mass of burnt dust in a crucible, weighing it, writing down the grammes and milligrammes, watching vaguely the bubbles coming up in the test-tubes fixed together with rubber joints. The blue flame of the burner danced its blue dance. 'Result', I wrote down in the big exercise book and added the two dots carefully.

'Equals?' The science mistress looked round, ignoring me in my stupidity.

The hand of the big round clock seemed scarcely to move at all. Now it stopped. Why so still? It must have stopped, at half past ten, just as my heart had missed a little beat.

'Now, for your homework I want you to . . .'

Everyone scribbled busily and then we filed out.

'Am I still playing Left Inner?' I asked as we all gathered round the notice-board to see the games chart.

'Oh, I should say so,' came my friend Diana's voice. 'We've got practice this afternoon and the match is next Saturday. We'll go up to the games field early, shall we?'

One! Two! Three! Our hockey sticks clicked. I caught the ball and held it, dribbled it down the field and passed it to Diana who picked it up and sped down the centre of the pitch; her auburn hair, in waves down her back, floated shining in the wind and sun. We came in at the goal, slicing the ball, and it hurtled away upon its own revolution, straight, dead on the mark . . .

School was when one was someone else and, above all, like all the other girls, as like as one could possibly manage.

Then the journey home, and at six o'clock at night I would walk into the kitchen with:

'Hello, Rue! What did you have for lunch?'

On that day Ruby was standing on the other side of the kitchen table polishing the silver.

'Liver pie. Lovely it was. Really lovely. I put yours in the oven.'

'Mmm.' A divine smell curled to my nostrils, wafted by appetite and imagination. Then I remembered the garage was empty of the car. 'When's she coming back?' There was always a hope that the gorgon would go away for days which could be like forever.

'She's been at the Norfolk and Norwich hospital. Mr Murry was operated on this morning.'

'Dadda?' Lumps of fear stuck in my throat. My mind flew back to the clock above the chemistry formulae.

'Yes,' said Ruby, 'at half past ten.'

After a month my father came home again. The sympathectomy which had been performed on the ganglion nerve was one of the first operations of its kind in the country. The internecine struggles with Betty at Larling were killing him, that much was certain, turning his legs to stone so that he could never escape. The weaker he became the greater was the destruction. Meanwhile Betty fed him with tender forced rhubarb and lightly boiled eggs.

When I saw him his head and trunk were sunk back upon the snow-white pillows. I stood fearfully at the foot of the bed, fearful before the total exhaustion of this man, my father, of his remoteness in his exhaustion.

'Hello, Dadda . . .'

But there was just the heavy breathing that used to disturb me when, as a very little girl, I would crawl into his bed in the early morning and wait for him to wake up. Why did he have to make so much noise, I would wonder as his chest heaved up and down, in and out, like a gigantic pair of bellows?

Now, standing there I waited, not daring to speak again.

'Hand me my milk, darling, will you?'

I held the glass, with the cream sitting nobly on top, to his lips.

Big Puss limped into the bedroom, her front paw scarcely healed after being caught again in a snare, and prepared to leap.

'Puss! No! No!' I whispered fiercely.

'What?'

'It's all right, Dadda. It's nothing. Only Puss.'

My father fell back to sleep again, the bellows in steady motion. All was well and I tiptoed out of the room.

17

Crises

'Dadda, when will the crisis be over?'

My father was sitting in the summer-house one summer morning in 1939. I was just off to school.

'I don't know, darling,' he said. 'I don't know. We might not be able to get over this one.'

'The last one blew over. Don't you remember?'

He shook his head. 'It may not be the same this time.'

'What . . . do you mean . . . we could have a war?'

'I'm afraid so.'

All at once everything seemed very still. The thatched summer-house, with its memories of bows and arrows; the rockery with the aubrieta and the pink saxifrage on its delicate stems and, under my feet, the blades of dewy grass. Would all this be gone, under tanks and guns in the smoke and stench of death?

My father was addressing an envelope.

'Post this for me on your way to school. Now you won't forget, will you?'

Only too happy to be of use to him, I slipped the letter into my blazer pocket.

Of late he had quite often asked this of me. I knew it was a secret but that did not worry me. My knowledge of his adult world limited itself to one simple and reassuring fact: namely that he was always right. I did not even know that, during the previous year, convalescing with friends in Wales, he had suffered a severe nervous breakdown. I would not, at fourteen, have understood the meaning of such a thing . . .

At this time Betty seemed a little calmer. Not that her dislike of me diminished, but I realised there was nothing I could do about it. Col would win her with his charm, Mêh with her peremptory demands, but my efforts required strategy which nearly always ended in collapse. Might she be going away for the weekend? I plotted with Ruby. Our hopes would soar. Soon we would toss pancakes and have sugar in our tea . . . But then, at the last minute, she would change her mind.

My father, often away now speaking at pacifist meetings up and down the country, seemed more remote somehow, less exasperated by her scenes, mild and unattainable.

Then, on 1st September, German tanks swept into Poland and the Luftwaffe dive-bombed the Polish airfields and Warsaw. Two days later, we in Britain were at war.

At Larling we made black-out curtains and prepared to receive a dozen evacuees. Bodge was in the Home Guard. My uncle Richard joined the Navy as a Commando and started his picture commentary of the War.

At school Miss Wood, our new headmistress, had an air-raid shelter dug into her lawn and, at the sound of a bell, gravely supervised as we practised filing in silence from our classrooms and taking up our positions along the benches in the dug-out with our gas masks and emergency rations.

Then, on the international scene, there was a lull. It was the time of the 'phoney' war. My father was even hopeful that Hitler might not dare to attack.

A weird tranquillity seemed to descend upon Larling, too, as if the house were living through its own 'phoney' war. Betty's outbursts seemed briefer and her discontent more diffused.

So when, one December evening in 1939, I arrived back from school and Betty greeted me with, 'Your father's gone off with another woman!', I was totally unprepared. I shook my head, speechless, merely staring at her.

'Oh yes he has, your wonderful father, off with another whore!'

'You are making a mistake. It's not true. I don't believe it.'

'Mistake? Look at this!' Betty pushed a letter at me with her shaking hand. 'Go on, look at it! Read it!' I could only stare the more at the blue envelope.

'Read it!'

But stubbornly I turned away from her and, wanting only to be alone, ran from the room, out of doors, into the back-yard. Above me the bare trees were soughing and the dark sky was starless.

'God, God,' I wept, 'let this not be true! Dadda, tell me, say it isn't true!'

I looked up. The sky, the dim clouds, the black branches all seemed to be reeling in some mad dance. I wandered over the cobble-stones. The windows of the box-rooms where we gave our plays, those of the pantry and larder below, the scullery and wash-room were all blacked out.

This house, so fearful with its tyrant and yet so dear, had somehow to be preserved intact. With this resolution I wiped my tears. Besides, there was no doubt whatsoever, Dadda would dispel Betty's ridiculous accusations, Col would soon be home for the Christmas holidays with Mêh running after him as usual and, above all, there was David, eighteen months now, staggering about, hanging onto my hand or putting his arms round my neck . . . I must warn Dadda, so that he could put everything right. Yes, tomorrow when I would see him on the train . . .

Armed with these comforting thoughts, I lifted the heavy latch of the back door and went into the kitchen where Ruby was spreading herself a slice of bread with beef dripping and sprinkling it with salt.

'Coo, she's taken on somethin' terrible today,' she whispered, 'She's been all through 'is desk. Everythin's on the floor.'

'But how did it start, Rue?'

'A letter came for 'im today. Then she started screamin' an' hit por little David.'

I produced a penny bar of Nestlé's chocolate from the slot machine on Thetford station and gave it to David who was watching us with large grey eyes.

'It'll all be fixed tomorrow, Rue, when Dadda comes back. It's all a lot of rubbish. Anyway, things have been better lately. He'd have no reason.'

I did not tell her of my clandestine meetings with him on the train. We heard Betty's footsteps and our conversation turned to generalities:

'Rue, have you seen my gas mask?'

'No. Lost it again have yer?'

'Must have left it in the train.'

'I'd like ter join the ATS. But I can't.'

'Why not?'

'Well, ter begin with, I can't leave Mr Murry an' the children. An' the second reason bein' I ain't tall enough.'

'That settles it, then, you've got to stay with us. Anyway Dadda says there may not be a proper war.'

'I might be allowed in the NAAFI, though, that's what they said,' said Ruby wistfully . . .

On the following day, on my way home, I left the school carriage where the girls were pulling down the blinds to make a mirror to re-arrange their hair, and went along the corridor to the London coaches. There, alone in the corner, sat my father, his face very pale and drawn under his soft grey trilby.

'Hello, Dadda.'

He started. 'Oh, hello, darling,' he said smiling. 'And how are things?'

'Dadda.' I paused, loath to upset him. 'You must be careful. Betty's been awful, talking a lot of rubbish.'

'Oh?' he sighed wearily. 'What sort of rubbish?'

'Well . . . she's been saying you . . . you . . .' I stumbled, 'that there's somebody else.'

Then I told him about the letter.

'Of course I said to her that it's all a mistake,' I went on, 'but she won't listen.' I paused and drew my breath and minutes went by before I could utter what was tormenting me:

'It's not true, is it, Dadda?'

My father looked at me very calmly and then spoke clearly and gently, with no hesitation:

'It is true. I must tell you this. I am sorry, my darling. You are too young to understand now but one day you will.'

I did not say, 'But why now? What about David? What about us all?' He was right. I did not understand. I searched his face, every line, the eyes, deep worlds, adult worlds.

'Without this I could not go on any more,' he was saying, half to himself.

The train slowed down. We were nearing our station. I had to leave him and go back to the school carriage. I kissed him.

'Look out, Dadda, won't you,' I said hastily. Nothing more. I did not want to question him. In my love, as in that of a little animal, there was no question.

18

War

In the summer of 1940, when the 'phoney' war had come to an end and Hitler over-ran Europe and the Battle of Britain raged, my father would take the train to London for half the week to edit *Peace News*. Physically fearless, he worked through the Blitz, refusing to go down to a shelter during the raids, his frailty alone preventing him from joining the rescue squads. Pacifists must not be suspected of cowardice, he would say, they must take on the most dangerous jobs. Often he would pay tribute to his country for allowing him to be a pacifist while it was fighting for its life. He stuck to his pacifism until he learned, years later, of the Jewish holocaust.

At Larling we led at times an 'Alice in Wonderland' existence. A detective arrived to go through my father's papers while the village constable kept him under surveillance. My father later described him:

> He sat, with his helmet in his hands, patiently watching me at my carpentry, keeping up official dignity for a while. Then the situation became too much for him. He suddenly grinned from ear to ear. 'The silly buggers!' he said. And I knew with relief that the heart of Britain was sound. I felt that, even if Hitler did win the Battle of Britain, Nazism could never subjugate the spirit of the people.*

It was on another such day that we had visitors—Rayner Heppenstall, 'Hepp' as we called him, and at the same time a shy young man, Geoffrey Sinclair, who had met my father at an ILP† meeting

---

* *Looking Before and After*, 1948 (Sheppard Press).
† Independent Labour Party.

in Norwich some years before and, on his advice, had joined the
Royal Air Force.

Over breakfast Hepp helped himself liberally to our butter ration.

'Enough of that,' snapped Betty. 'You conchies and spongers!
Leave the butter for the ones that fight! Here you are, Geoffrey, help
yourself!'

The embarrassed Geoffrey had been watching David, perched up
on cushions at the table beside my father who was deep in *The
Times*, oblivious of his little son carefully spooning tea from his
father's cup into his jacket pocket . . .

But where was our laughter, oh where? It would be many, many
years before we would recall such things with gaiety. Many years
before I could recall anything at all . . .

My father spent more time now at the Adelphi Centre at Langham. He was trying to reach a *modus vivendi* with Betty which
would permit him to keep Larling and his children together and at
intervals to find the love and support elsewhere which Betty could
not give him.

As in the affair with Nehale, he even conceived that Betty and his
lady should become friends, and his ideas as to how to achieve such
a thing were, as I see it now, hilarious. The trouble was that Betty
had no sense of humour and my father entirely overlooked the bare
fact that no woman would share him.

He arranged the meeting away from Larling. But Betty made
short shrift of it and returned home precipitously, interrupting
Ruby's and my joyous relief at her departure. Her reaction, regret-
tably, was so violent, her descriptions of her rival so lurid, that all
our hopes of future peace were completely shattered.

Larling was now becoming an eerie phantom house, real only in
its terrible reality to those who lived under its roof. Hidden in its
plantations, who could know its unhappy secret? This woman who
did her weekly shopping and was so uneccentric in appearance, who
realised she had moments of uncontrollable fury? Mrs Middleton
Murry.

One day, when the birds were singing with very clear notes, as if
the raindrops they announced were already in their throats, Betty's
voice echoed through the house.

All that day and the following day. All that night and the
following night:

'You take your two children and I'll take mine!'

And: 'I'll keep Larlin', darlin'.'

And: 'You get out and go to the old c . . .'

Suddenly there was a cry, of a wild, lonely despair. A great cry coming from a heart bursting with grief. A man's cry.

Ashes of fear were in my mouth, sticking round my tongue. I was kneeling on a rug on the lawn with David who was stretching his arm towards our old cat, moulting, lame, with her torn ear.

Doors were banging. I heard the unmistakable step over the sill of the french window, the faint swish of grass underfoot, and Betty's voice:

'Don't you touch him! You take your hands off my child. Give him to me at once. You go where you belong! You get out! You go with your father!'

David, caught up, swung in mid-air by this force which was his mother, began to whimper, turning his eyes upon me in wonderment.

'Now don't you start!' she said, pressing him tight against her under her arm, as if back into her womb, and turned quickly, walking with abrupt staccato steps, her whole body taut. She crossed the lawn, crackled over the gravel drive and disappeared.

I went indoors but everything seemed empty, like a hollow shell. Holes of darkness here and there. A breeze blew up into a draught and banged another door.

'Dadda!'

I ran upstairs. The voice had come from there. The voice I had heard on the lawn.

'Dadda!'

On his bed were the black air stockings he wound round his legs, the red rubber tubes, all his paraphernalia awry, the little wooden shelf with its brass hooks dangling, caught in the bed-clothes.

'Dadda! Dadda!'

Now unformed terror gave me wings.

Along the landing to the bathroom. I opened the door. He was there.

'Oh . . .!' I stepped forward, my hand out to touch him. He started. Was he dreaming? He was so white, so strange.

'Shall I get you your medicine, Dadda?' But which, for God's sake?

My eyes ran over the bottles.

'The black . . .' His voice was behind me as I peered into the cupboard. The black medicine. We children were half convinced of its magic powers. He kept it in a big bottle. It was made up at the chemist's to Jimmy Young's special formula: one tablespoonful to be taken when necessary. Very special. Like the ear-wigs he would pretend to eat in his apples. Only my father could eat and drink such things to do him good!

He drank it down and after a while laughed shortly:

'Well! That was a near one!'

What did he mean? I did not ask, but waited patiently. He got up, and I followed him. At a little distance. Downstairs. I was using the forbidden front stairs but it did not matter: the house was empty and somehow everything was subtly different. Just him and me. 'Hah!' Again the short, queer laugh. I was still behind him as he crossed the hall to his study. Betty had gone over to the Hewetsons' with David and Mary.

I had waited all day to tell him. So I followed him. Now surely was the time to please him.

'Dadda . . . I've passed.'

'Passed?' He was vague as he drew out his chair to sit at his desk.

'My exams. I've passed them.'

'Why, that's good news . . .'

But I knew he had not really registered the information, so important to me, and I stood there feeling I ought to go and leave him, yet disappointed.

'You said if I did we'd . . . we'd celebrate.'

'Ah?'

'That's what you said.'

He pulled some papers towards him. I put my arm round his shoulder and kissed him.

'Here,' he said, 'have a humbug,' and he opened his tin of Parkinson's Peppermint Humbugs.

'Thank you, Dadda.' It was a precious gift endowed with a special ritual. Diamonds could not have been more prized. Then, remembering what I had told him, he said again:

'That *is* good news, darling.' He paused, then suddenly looked up at me with a wink: 'I'll tell you what? Let's *celebrate*!'

'Celebrate? Now?'

He grinned, like a schoolboy. 'Let's have some wine!' and cocking an eyebrow, 'Shall we?'

'Oh yes!' But I was a bit nervous.

We glided into the empty drawing-room like a couple of thieves: with his finger to his lips, he turned the key to the glass-paned cupboard where the port and sherry were kept.

'Fetch some glasses.'

I ran to the kitchen and brought back what I thought were the prettiest, with gold rims.

He poured out from one of the bottles a liquid that glowed red-amber in the setting sun.

'Here's to better times!' He raised his glass and smiled.

'Do you think it will be better?' I asked. I could not envisage it.

'It will be better, I am sure,' he said.

It could certainly hardly have been worse.

'Do you think we'll be happy? One day?' I asked again.

'Why, yes. Perhaps sooner than you think.'

I suspected him of saying this to please me and sipped the wine dutifully. I did not like it but did not tell him, so as not to spoil our moment.

'That one day we can go away?' I went on, thinking of Shelley's green isle.

The blackbirds were still singing, their lovely clarity intensified by the evening stillness. Long shadows were growing over the lawn. The future. Happiness. It hung, suspended in my imagination like a golden island. Rocking in the liquid in our glasses.

He seemed to give my question his serious and considered reflection. I waited. The conspiracy we shared made even the waiting a delight.

The wine, daring and strange, seemed to stretch an invisible antenna into the future, even as it was held in my father's hand.

'Yes,' he said at length—and he seemed positive—'I'm sure, darling, it will end happily ever after. Now go and wash the glasses and don't tell anyone.'

A short time later, my father left Larling for good and Betty once more threw his clothes out after him.

19

The Cost

'Is it better,' my father had asked me, 'when I am away?'

I admitted that Betty was less violent and it was better therefore for Mêh and David. So when the final break came and in 1941, for the second time in five years, a van took away his desk and books to the Adelphi Centre, I was at least thankful for his safety.

He arranged with Miss Wood at school to correspond with me there. His letters I kept in my desk, but at the end of the term I took them back with me to Larling where I hid them in my room. Betty found and burned them. But I remember he always wrote that he would never desert me while allowing me a free choice of whether or not I would leave Larling.

It was David who prevented me. Or rather, my love for the little boy. I recall taking him for walks in the walled garden and watching while he splashed the pools of rain trapped in the rhubarb leaves. Past the strawberry cage we would go and through the green door in the wall, keeping at a respectful distance from the bee-hives on the edge of the paddock, then through a wooden gate and up the beech avenue.

'Do you like spiders, Weg?'

'Little ones. They are lucky. Not the big black ones.'

'Weg?'

'Yes.'

'Why is Mummy cross with you?'

We had come to the end of the beech walk. There was a wire fence beyond and, westwards, we could see a big plantation in the middle of the field where the spring wheat was sprouting tender green. We could have been on the edge of the world.

'I don't know, Dave.' The breeze caught up my words and wafted them away. Then I added with a tang of venom:

'She's always getting cross about something or other, anyway.'

But David seemed untouched.

'Why doesn't she like you, Weg?' He was swinging with one foot on the wire fence, to and fro with the rusty wire screeching monotonously.

'Why, Weg?' he insisted. The nape of his neck was white beneath his fair curls.

I thought for a moment but I had no answer.

We went round the orchard and Lumley's hay barn and into our cobbled yard. Smoke was puffing out of one of the chimneys at the back of the house. That morning Bodge had lit the boiler in the wash-room. We went indoors, watched the red glow and listened to the roar of the furnace, smelled the steam rising up from the boiling sheets. Betty's arms were trembling with pent-up delirium that would churn and churn as the morning went on, churn itself into paroxysm, even as she churned the sheets in the dolly, pulling the wooden handle back and forth so that the propeller inside whipped up the water and the soap suds and the linen. The round dolly strained and moaned on its three legs with their iron castors, and then the clean washing was pushed through the mangle and pulled out flat the other side.

'Now you give me that there 'ere, Mrs Murry.'

Gently Bodge took over the handle from her and continued its motion with ease, scarce swaying at the hips.

'An unpaid housekeeper. That's all I am. Here, give me over the blue,' said Betty as she snatched it from Bodge.

And the clear water swirled with the blue-bag driven by her white hand.

'He can take his two children. I'll keep mine. He's not going to have mine!'

Water gushed from the soft water pump into the stone sink. The window was steamed up. The wicker clothes basket filled. A trickle of soapy water ran over the red brick floor.

'Come on, Dave, let's go out again and see Taffy.'

Taffy was the Welsh pony we kept to cart wood from the plantations for our winter fires.

'Want a pig-a-back? Come on, then, up you get!' I crouched

down on all fours and heaved him up on my back where he hung onto my neck as we visited Taffy grazing stoutly in the swing-tree meadow.

'Taffy! Taffy! Come here, girl, come on!' Taffy was indifferent to my coaxing. We moved closer but she cut a caper and cantered away into the next paddock, past the hen-run with our fifteen red-brown biddies squawking their upset, to where Betty was now standing pegging out, with stiff, angular movements, the billowing white sheets.

Since it was wash day she had to be avoided even more than usual, but David, oblivious of such precautions, whimpered on seeing his mother.

'Now stop that!' cried Betty.

David began to cry.

'Now stop it!'

He responded with loud bawls.

'Get him out of my sight!' And Betty clipped him over the ear. 'Take him away. Go and feed him. And don't let me catch you using the front stairs . . .'

David's grey eyes clouded, his face puckered. But I could not know then that my fears for him, far from being groundless, were to be cruelly borne out.

I live to portray the meadows, the woods, the beauty and tranquillity that surrounded the terrible Old Rectory, an island in the middle of a lake and the lake lapping on the shores of the outer world. Warily I would scout round eyeing the dark windows, sometimes taking David on my back, and wondering whom I had the right to love.

The little boy was tender. He grew up to forget everything—as both his sisters forgot—but worse: a great growing blank in his mind that there was no way out of, a cancer of a blank. But in the back of his eyes remained a strange purity. To the end.

He was sent to the best schools, but he could not carry on and, after my father died, he abandoned his training at a naval college and drifted into the world of ne'er-do-wells and people on the make. Finally, while working as a driver for a petrol company, the tanker he was driving exploded. He was twenty-two.

Do we in the end forgive everything—from tiredness or an old fear of rejection? Do we ever forgive the fate of David? What does it matter to him now, anyway?

But it matters to us. In the débacle when all was broken up at Larling, David was sacrificed.

*   *   *

The great elms that had sighed and sorrowed over me that winter's night when I had stood in the yard gazing up at the blackening sky, crying for help, might have seen me, two years later, still hoping: if Betty would learn to master her violence then, I thought, all would be well again. Again? No. All would be well for the first time. Betty would have acquired self-control, our father would return and David would grow up strong and healthy and beautiful, well taught and guided into manhood.

My father had gone but Larling still endured: its subterfuge, its obscenities, its trickeries—*my* trickery. The destructiveness of it.

One day, in the dining room, Betty's face looked up at me:

'You, Weg,' she said, 'you write and tell him to come back to us. If *you* write . . .'

Her face was stained with tears, imploring me.

All at once I saw her simply as another woman, a woman whose husband had left her and her two small children, the house empty of the man. For a moment it seemed her tempers did not mean anything, that they were just mistakes. I loved her. No longer with the little girl's yearning love but with the compassion of an adult, of one who suddenly found herself the stronger.

Perhaps he would come back . . . perhaps . . . and give it another try, mend this 'broken home'. If I asked? Come back, Dadda, from the foreign, outer world.

What was that world when all I could see was this tear-stained face, thin gash of a mouth, the hair dyed to a pathetic keeping with a mythical thirty-seven years, the legs grown thin and marked with brown network from the heat of the fire?

'Write it, lass, he'll listen to you,' she said.

Oh, the fatal word that spoke to my soul, the word her sister Dot had used when I was seven! Lass. Like a little bright star it leaped over a black void from years back. Irresistible.

And so I wrote. It was so simple, really; if my father would only see. I wrote and pleaded with him to come back to Betty.

Then I went and put David to bed.

My father was astonished and grieved. Although I cannot remember whether he replied, he must have thought, '*Et tu, Brute?*'

20

End of an Era

I was now a virtual prisoner at Larling, partly through my own volition in caring for David, but mainly through Betty's jealousy. She could not allow me friends or contacts outside her own orbit or understanding. This meant none at all.

When I was sixteen, however, Miss Winifred Trimby, who was familiar with our situation, generously extended to me her devoted admiration for my father and invited me to her home in Welwyn Garden City. It was the first time I had been away on my own since my Belgian visit five years previously. Betty grudgingly let me go.

After an enchanted week when I was freed from anxiety and surrounded with affection, my father arranged that I should meet him at Liverpool Street station on my way back to Larling. This was the crowning point of my holiday and my heart was light with expectation. It was many months since I had seen him and I missed him sorely.

In the cafeteria where we met I hurried towards him. He kissed me and then said:

'This is Mary.'

Those three words only.

He turned towards a lady in black sitting at his table. I had not noticed her or, in the crowded buffet, connected her with him. My surprise was so complete at this unexpected encounter with the very person Betty so vilified that, as on so many occasions, I was tongue-tied.

I stared at her black veiled hat and her many rings. This person bore no resemblance at all to Betty's hideous descriptions and none either to our simple, almost spartan life at Larling.

My father then made me a present of *Nicholas Nickleby*. I

thanked him and fell silent with confusion and shyness. I was dimly aware that he was making me take a leap in initiation for which I was totally unprepared. The visit to Miss Trimby, Betty might eventually accept. This meeting, never. Why had he not warned me?

These thoughts crowded my mind but outweighing them all was, I confess, the desperate urge to break out into hysterical laughter, although I saw nothing funny in the situation at all.

I cannot remember our conversation, only the dim smoke-filled cafeteria, the chink of cups, the hum of many voices, the smell of fish arriving from Yarmouth and my attempts to suppress this dreadful desire to laugh.

Alas, I could not and the guilt I felt towards Betty for having met her rival was only equalled by that towards my father for such shocking behaviour. As I fingered the shiny cellophane cover of my book, I longed for release.

At last it was time for my train. The lady came along the platform to see me safely into the carriage.

I was grateful to her. She had been kind. Grateful, too, because my father was safe and happy now. But deep within my being I felt the weight of a knowledge I could not express. It was not of time nor experience but it was in my very veins, in the flesh that was myself as I stood at the open window looking down into her light-blue eyes.

My father had left Larling for ever.

It seemed at that moment that I was the older woman. Time seemed to have taken me up, years and perhaps centuries. Like a river it flowed under my feet. I had nobody. My physical body, my skin that felt the silken half-prickle of the artificial silk lining of my coat, seemed without any weight, borne along by that invisible river, even part of the river itself.

The stranger (who was eventually to become my father's fourth wife) was doing all she could, I knew. But she could not do all. Don't worry, I wanted to say, don't break your heart over trying.

'Shall you be all right?' She looked up at me anxiously and put her hand up on the wooden frame of the window. The leather strap pressed against me as I stood there.

'Quite all right. And thank you. Don't worry,' I replied.

The train drew out. The river seemed to flow more and more quickly. I sat down in a corner and put my cheek against the carpet tufts of the head-rest that smelt of smoke. I felt weak and tired. The train was taking me to Larling. Yet I had nowhere to go.

I closed my eyes. We hurtled through a long tunnel. Then I looked out once more at the countryside rushing past, fresh and beautiful. Cows grazed beside ponds in lush meadows and beneath trees whose great branches cast a protective shade. Hedges of hawthorn glittered royally. Great white clouds swung in majesty over the blue sky, over the gentle rise and fall of the land, until the entire universe seemed to sway and tip, balanced in greatness, breathing so naturally in such harmony.

East Anglia.

Cambridge. Ely.

'Don't you know there's a war on?' a soldier shouted in the corridor. There was laughter and a clumping of boots and the dumping of army packs.

Ely. Thetford.

The old familiar scene. The train riding between the high banks, under the bridge. Each house, each familiar meadow and tree and the sound of the train itself, was always the same, in the same place.

Harling Road. This was it.

'Harlin' Road Sta-shun! Harlin' Road Sta-shun!' came the East Anglian lilt.

I opened the door and jumped down. The expanse of grey platform stretched a long way. I seemed to float through space, through nothingness, and felt the same old fear.

I walked down to the barrier. No one was there to meet me. Half relieved, half disappointed, I pushed open the wooden gate and started up the hill. The train drew out, gathered speed and disappeared behind the bend.

Then, in the distance, I saw a pram coming towards me and, pushing it, a small, stocky figure hurrying, bobbing up and down.

My heart leaped. 'Hi, Rue!' I cried.

Valiantly she came towards me, flushed beetroot.

'Rue! Hello, Rue!'

David was sitting there, blond and serious little boy.

'Dave!'

His hair shone downy, a gold-silver crest.

'How's the weather?' I asked anxiously.

Ruby strapped David more firmly into place and replied:

'She's been really terrible today. I've come ter warn yer. She's sure you've seen that other woman.'

Abruptly I stopped. There was nothing to say. I could not tell the truth. To hide my confusion I bent down to do up my shoe.

'Why on earth does she think that?' I said as we continued over the turn-pike and down the other side of the hill, and I prepared myself for what was to come.

'I dunno,' said Ruby, 'I'm jes warnin' yer.'

We neared the house. Mentally I rehearsed my lies, engulfed in fear yet outwardly composed.

In the kitchen Betty was standing on the far side of the big table. The convulsive trembling of her whole body exuded an electricity of delirium. In unspeakably foul language she accused me of having met my father and the 'other woman'. It was truly uncanny how she divined it, as if the intensity of hysteria within her had its own clairvoyance.

In reply to my false denials she picked up a knife lying on the table. The knife itself did not frighten me—it was not a very sharp one—but the waves of violence that surged from her certainly did. As she rushed at me, Bodge, whom Ruby had fetched, came in.

'Now you go upstairs, ol' dear,' he said, 'an' keep your door locked. I'll look after the Missus, else she'll be harmin' you, there ain't no doubt. She's really took on, she is.'

As I went upstairs I heard him quietly coaxing:

'Now you put that knife down, Mrs Murry. You ain't got no use fer that . . . Now give it ter me, then . . .'

Behind my locked door it did not occur to me that had I been brave and told Betty the truth from the outset, her reaction might conceivably have been better . . .

Then, as the months passed by at Larling, Betty seemed to let herself go and spent a lot of time in bed. Christmas was coming. Doggedly I decorated the tree and made mince-pies. Col arrived from school with his usual fund of tricks and jokes which, with great temerity, he sometimes played on Betty. We celebrated the day as best as we could. But Betty took no interest. Sometimes she would visit the airing cupboard and go through my father's best shirts that she was keeping so that he should not wear them with 'that old whore'.

As if from nowhere, a photograph appeared on her bedside table. Was it a brother of hers? There was talk of soldiers being billeted at the Rectory . . .

In January and February, in order to attend to my studies, I stayed in lodgings that Miss Wood had found for me in Thetford and only went home at weekends. Every Friday evening I would enquire with trepidation of Ruby or Bodge, how 'things' were, and I noticed David becoming more and more difficult before Betty's unpredictable ways.

Then—it was towards the end of March—as I was walking to Thetford station, I stopped abruptly in my tracks. I had no more reason than usual to drag my feet but today I choked at the humiliations and, above all, at the uselessness of trying to save David.

As if sleep-walking, I found myself going to Miss Wood's doorstep.

'Ring that bell or you will have lost your life forever!' I told myself sternly. 'Go on, press it or forever hold your peace!'

The round brown bell looked harmless enough, but behind it, I knew, was a precipice where I had to risk my all; if I did not, my life would be insidiously and incurably rotted to its core.

Perhaps it was that small kernel that Louise so long ago had nurtured in me, perhaps it was a surfeit of degradations at Larling, perhaps it was that I had simply grown up.

I pushed the bell.

It echoed loudly through the house.

Miss Wood herself came to the door.

'I am sorry to trouble you,' I ventured, 'but I . . . I can't go back any more.'

Her wise, grey-blue eyes were calm and did not betray a flicker of surprise.

'Why, come in, my dear,' she said gently, 'I have been waiting for this. Take your coat off and have some tea. I will telephone your father.'

On the following morning she took me over to Larling in her car to fetch my belongings. The house was empty. I went up to my bedroom. A suitcase was in the middle of the floor, the contents of my drawers and cupboard emptied into it. I hurried downstairs with it. We called at the Hewetsons'. Mr Hewetson gave me a box of double-yoked eggs and, in the shy way he had, wished me luck in the future. Then off we sped.

Betty's final onslaught came that afternoon. I was playing the part of Elizabeth in our school production of *Pride and Prejudice*. It was the dress rehearsal. Suddenly Betty irrupted into the back of the hall shouting obscenities and dragging poor Mêh behind her.

In my shame and embarrassment I managed to stay very calm as I said, haughtily, I suppose, 'I think we had better discuss this outside,' and came down from the stage. Betty made to strike me and followed me out through the doors. The tight Empire dress I was wearing was not intended for such feats and, as I lured her away from the hall, I picked up my skirts and ran like a frightened hare through the empty school to the inner door which connected with Miss Wood's house.

My father happened to be with her. Almost at once the outside door bell rang, that same bell I had pressed the evening before, and the maid opened it to Betty.

'Go upstairs to the little bedroom.' Miss Wood pushed me hurriedly. 'Don't come down until I fetch you.'

The scene I heard downstairs, Mêh's voice crying 'Mummy! Mummy!', the revelation to the rest of my class of my true family background which I had up until then so proudly concealed, all contributed to my impassioned desire to die.

I did not, of course. It was, however, the last time I saw Betty, the gorgon of my youth. My childhood was over.

*   *   *

Thus Larling, with its tribe of children that my father had wanted so much, was broken up. After I left he did not allow Col to go there, either, but Betty held on grimly to the house and to 'her' two children.

Court proceedings to obtain a divorce were undertaken by my father. Betty refused to free him or to allow him access to David and Mêh, and sued him for desertion—and all the money she could get. In those days divorce matters were even more sordid and interminable than they are today; years dragged on, with Betty bombarding my father with letters and telegrams of incoherent abuse, until she left Larling for a house in the shires. Ten years later she was to die suddenly of a brain haemorrhage. At long last my father was released.

Mêh, grown up, opted for security and married an insurance broker. A while ago, when she was ill with cancer, to distract her we would play our 'Do you remember?' game that she had always liked.

'Do you remember, Weg,' she said, 'how the three of us got into your big bed with you and you said we'd all be happy together one day?'

I smiled. I had forgotten, my heart wrung by her sad mouth. Mêh, who died so bravely before her time.

*   *   *

I have been writing this book abroad. During that time the cherry tree outside my window burst into flower, then lost its ripening fruit to the birds, and now its leaves are turning tawny gold.

I gaze at it and in my mind view England again, the gleaming white cliffs with their grassy caps; eastwards our holiday sand dunes with the many church spires; to the west the sandy bay of Barmouth and, down south, the Atlantic that pounds on the shingles in front of the Old Coastguard Station.

I see the Old Rectory, too. The house is now visible from quite far away. The new occupants have cut down many of its trees. The garden is trim and angular. The swing has gone from the great beech in the paddock.

Indoors, the scrubbed white table has gone as well, and the familiar stove; they are replaced by modern equipment. There is no longer the old grandfather clock in the hall or the Persian carpets which were my father's delight.

The grass is long in Hewetson's meadow. The chicken huts are closed. The bee-hives have been taken away, along with the printing press, and at the bottom of the drive a patterned wall of red and grey bricks has replaced the simple white palings.

The time has come for me to go forwards again. The house in the plantations recedes. The earth curves as, like some bird in flight, I leave it all behind.

And yet, for me, David's hand is eternally in mine; Mêh eternally runs to fetch and carry for Col; and Col, lost in concentration, with his tongue caught between his teeth, is still making tree-houses and kites and boats, while Ruby still cackles her laughter with Bodge, as he comes in, cap in hand, for his morning cocoa.

Overlooking the lawn from his study window, my father still sits at his desk, deep in thought. He draws a book over to him—one of his own, *Keats and Shakespeare*—picks up his pen and inscribes it with the words:

'Nothing ever becomes real until it is experienced.'

Epilogue

'To keep faith with the dead, who were pioneers, is to press on with their voyage of discovery . . . they give us strength; we give them life in return.' So my father wrote in 1944.*

So indeed he always pressed on with his voyages of discovery. Indifferent to building himself up into a public persona, this critic and moralist, poet and mystic, journalist and scholar, was the reverse of a success story.

Romantic, pure, innocent, like Cervantes' hero, he was a lone knight, too, of infinite courage: rich pasture for the cynic but for those who truly knew him, a gentleman beyond compare.

When, in 1957, he was dying in hospital (I had left the family for a moment at the hotel nearby and come to sit by his bed) I found myself saying (the words were not premeditated but direct from my heart), 'We do adore you so, Dadda,' and he replied, simply and quietly: 'I know, my precious.'

Beside him was a novel of Trollope's and some notes.

The throbbing vein that ran down the side of his neck was agonisingly swollen as his worn-out body struggled in the long, long nightmare between life and death. He would look at me as if to say: 'What a mess, darling. How can I get out of this?', just as he had always looked at me, knowing I knew.

But he died serenely, alone in the night, in full possession of himself. The battles were over. The happiness that had been his during his last years with Mary Gamble, his fourth wife, had been his paradise on earth.

He did not want his life prolonged to become an invalid. Besides,

* *Adam and Eve*, 1944 (Dakers).

he was exhausted. 'Katherine would have let me go,' he said. The freedom he gave Katherine he was asking for now. Freedom to go in peace.

He was buried in the village graveyard. A few of us, family and friends, were in the church for the burial service. The little carrier that bore the coffin up the aisle was like an old-fashioned pram with its big wheels, and how small the plain oak coffin looked. Like an offering of innocence to a yearning and lonely God.

Index